THE FREEDOM BUS

BY JENNY ROSSITER

FROM ADOPTION
TO TRUE SELF

Published by Feel Good Leadership Limited
in the UK

Edited and designed by:
Memorandum Company Histories
15 Keynote Studios
62–72 Dalmain Road
London
SE23 1AT
020 8133 6588
memocoh.com

*To my Mum and Dad for always believing in me
and showing me what love really means*

*Thanks to all of the people in my life for loving
and supporting me along my journey, and my
ancestors for making it all possible*

CONTENTS

Part 2

PREFACE

Dare to Discover

This is a book about loss, hope and adventure. But, most of all, it's about a little girl who—despite an unusual beginning—had the determination to make her life better. Beneath the feelings of shame, rejection and pain that came with being adopted, she had lost the love for, and connection with, herself, although she never lost her sense of adventure. On her journey of self-discovery, she has explored her past, examined her present and reconnected with her dreams for the future. Through this personal enquiry in midlife, she has been empowered to be her true self. This book is about the freedom self-discovery brings.

As an adoptee, my search for understanding myself was perhaps greater than most. Even so, it's a journey many people need to make. Within the book, I write not only from my personal perspective but as a corporate leadership coach, sharing the process I take my clients through to help them make sense of their situations and so find solutions to their biggest questions.

So, who is this book for?

You might be a wonderful mother, a busy CEO, an adoptee, or even an adoptee with ADHD, like me. You may well be successful and have a reasonably *happy* life, but you might just be itching to have a more *meaningful* life.

You might have achieved a lot, but it's been hard, you've overworked, worn yourself out and got to a point where your life feels like a slog and you've lost sight of the point.

You might feel trapped in a job with no time to play, stuck in a role that is more like a hamster wheel than a profession. You might have lost meaning or just feel as flat as a pancake. Life is restricting and a hard place to be.

Regardless of our circumstances, none of is are immune from the pain of being human or the desire to just be true to you.

I was little Pollyanna, grateful and happy for everything but secretly crying myself to sleep. I had squashed my feelings of loss, grief and shame so deeply that I didn't know they existed. I spent many years hiding how I felt because I was embarrassed to say that this successful woman was sometimes sad inside and wasn't always coping as expected.

Whatever is happening, you may not feel free to be yourself. But there is always a way out, however bad it's got. Through deep exploration on my journey, I have found a version of myself that I didn't know existed.

We all have our own bus to freedom. We just have to see it.

Through the work I have done, and through writing this book, I have been on a deep journey of personal understanding, connection and compassion. Looking back and reassessing my life has enabled me to discover my true self. I have connected the different aspects of myself and have become whole. With true understanding, I see that I am more capable than I ever thought I was. I will never again let shame or rejection get in the way of who I am or who I am about to become.

I never want any child to be ashamed of feeling the way they do because there is no shame in being you. I have told my personal story, but pain is universal. We all experience loss, trauma and hurt. I hope that anyone reading this book sees that it's never too late to be yourself and that the world truly is your oyster.

At 52, I have never been more deeply grateful for the life I have. Thank you for taking the time to read my story. I wish you and your family much happiness and joy.

The bus is round the corner. Don't be late!

PART 1

MY STORY: REJECTION TO ACCEPTANCE

CHAPTER 1

MY THREE FAMILIES

Searching for a Sense of Belonging

I had an uncertain and unusual start, to say the least.

I was born on 6 March 1969 at St Mary's Hospital in London to Lorraine Vera Ching, a New Zealander of Anglo-Maori background, and given up for adoption soon afterwards. This was to have three profound effects on me.

Firstly, it would prove to me how deeply embedded our genes are. Regardless of what would happen to me in my life, having Maori connections always felt important. Some of my birth mother's ancestors were Cornish, but I've always felt more of a Kiwi or tribal South Seas Islander than a woman rooted in my white British ancestry.

This cultural link can be traced to 1841 when the Chings—in the shape of Richard and his wife Jane—left

7

Cornwall bound for the Antipodes, to better themselves. They finally set foot in Nelson (and were among the earliest migrants to do so), and the Ching family, particularly my great-great-great-great grandfather William, became highly respected members of the farming community there. In 2020, seeing a photo of him and the Ching family for the first time was profound. It gave me a sense of my heritage, of where I had come from.

The second impact of my shaky start and subsequent adoption was that it eventually gave me a feeling of being different, unique even, and with this a certain sense of strength as I made my way in the world.

The third effect was that my birth mother, Lorraine, whose mother was Rata Tui Ching (Rata is the name of a beautiful New Zealand tree and Tui is a colourful bird with mystical powers), qualified as a nurse. My birth mother's choice of career influenced me greatly, and nursing would play a big part in my life.

My Birth Parents

At 23, Lorraine came to the UK on a career break to gain overseas experience. She nursed for a while in London before taking a job as a secretary to my birth father, Peter Gerald Allen, a 41-year-old coin dealer with offices in Great Portland Street, and, it turns out, a real character. Peter's early story mirrored my own. His mother decided that she could only look after his brothers, and he was placed in an orphanage. His grandmother was the only one to offer him love and she, in turn, was so poor that she could barely afford to eat, often sharing a banana with my birth father—and she would eat the skin.

Against such a poverty-stricken background, it was no surprise that Peter strove to get on in life. He made money, enjoyed it and eventually gave much of it away to the poor. He became known in business as 'Maundy Allen' because he specialised in Maundy money—coins issued each year to the poor of a parish by The Queen on the day before Good Friday. Peter's expertise and fame extended to the royal family, and over the years he even met the Queen Mother!

Peter was a flamboyant, cigar-smoking, wine-drinking man about town, used to frequenting Soho clubs, mixing with the crowd at the Raymond Revuebar (owned by 'King of Soho' Paul Raymond). He was married to Irene (known as Neddy), and they lived in Dorset Square, near Baker Street, London with a second home in Devon. They had no children.

As happens in work situations, Lorraine had an affair with Peter, and I was the result. Unhappily for him, Peter had fallen in love, but despite their relationship and Lorraine's pregnancy, it became clear that Lorraine did not share his feelings and romantic intentions. Peter did not realise this at the time as she said that she needed to return to New Zealand to explain the situation to her family, during which time Peter told Neddy that he was leaving her for his newfound love.

Thinking all was well, and as was his wont, Peter drove to Heathrow in a flash car to meet Lorraine on her return, only to be told that she did not want to marry him. "And you are too irresponsible to look after the baby, which I am going to have adopted," she added.

This was tremendously sad for Peter. An orphan himself, he had no children with Neddy and now faced losing both Lorraine, the love of his life, and his one and only daughter— me. After Peter lost Lorraine and the possibility of a child, feeling desolate, he gave up his London business and left his marital home, never to return. He consoled himself by sailing off around the world looking for rare coins ("lost treasure"), celebrating each find with a bottle of champagne.

Peter and Neddy never lived together again, but they remained good friends until the day he died. In his loyal and gentlemanly way, Peter always looked after his wife so that, in her cosy Dorset Square flat, she never wanted for a thing.

Given up for Adoption

While in New Zealand, 24-year-old, pregnant Lorraine pondered the fact that her whole life was in front of her. During this time, she also met and fell in love with her future husband and the father of my half brother and sister.

She must have concluded that she did not fancy sharing her life with an older, divorced man who hung out in Soho smoking cigars. But in deciding to have the baby, and giving me up for adoption, she ensured that I had a life— and with it the chance of being brought up in a safe and reliable home.

Anyway, there I was, on 11 March 1969, five days after my birth, in local authority care in Yateley near Sandhurst, cared for by Mrs Denton, whom I would only ever know by name and address. Every instinct, however, tells me that she was kind. Although she is probably no longer alive, I would like to say thank you to Mrs Denton, who looked after me in the first three months of my life.

A Little Warm Nest
—My First Year of Life

During my three months in Mrs Denton's cosy cottage, from March to June 1969, I was about to have a stroke of luck. Elsewhere in Hampshire, Brian and Jean from Southampton were looking to find a new child.

In families who adopt, it is often the loss of a baby or unrealised fertility that triggers the search for a new life. There is a surplus of love and a little warm nest that is so often already meant for someone else.

The Rossiters already had my brother Ian and had sadly lost their second son in a devastating and deeply sad turn of events. I would be chosen to move into the Rossiter family to be loved in his place. So, as Graham was lost, I was found, and I gained a mum and dad—and for that, I will always be grateful.

23 June 1969 was my 'New Home Day'. I was handed over to Mum and Dad, and they were given guardianship of a new baby. I must have been on my best behaviour as on 9 July 1969, my parents made an application to adopt me and keep me forever. For six months I was under the watchful eyes of the social workers. Then, on 29 January 1970, my

mum and dad paid the humble sum of £1 to Southampton County Court for me to legally become a Rossiter.

Being monitored by social services is one thing but, to make matters worse, on 26 February Baby Ching almost became Baby Allen. Peter wasn't giving up his quest to keep his daughter and went to court with Neddy to claim me. I don't know the details, and can't imagine the trauma for him, but on 12 March 1970, the judge made an order: "Jenny Elizabeth Ching, you are now Jenny Elizabeth Rossiter and an official member of the Rossiter family."

The Three Magic Words:
"We Chose You"

As I settled into family life with the Rossiters in Chandler's Ford, on the northern edge of Southampton, they made me aware early—certainly before I was five—that I was adopted. I don't remember not knowing. Mum said that I was really special: "We chose you." These were three magic words to me and, indeed, at primary school I wore this phrase like a badge of honour, boasting: "I am adopted, and my parents chose me!"

Mum's best friend, Auntie Campbell, tried to burst my bubble later on when she quietly told me that this was not true and that my mum was in a panic as she had been given a girl with a shock of red hair who didn't look like her!

None of this mattered to little Jenny, who still wore her boastful badge which announced to the world: I'm special, I'm chosen and aren't I the lucky one! That reassuring message would have a profound effect on me in later years, reinforcing feelings of my difference and encouraging a spirit of independence in me.

Life in the Rossiter family was wonderful in so many ways although, as with all special gifts, you don't realise this until you look back at it with fresh eyes. I had a loving home with Brian and Jean in their bungalow in middle-class England with its long garden—lots of space for me to play and run around.

Jean was one of those mums who was always there and never really went anywhere. She was up in the morning and ready with breakfast and waiting at night when, in the terrifying darkness, I shouted out: "Muummmy... I'm scared. Please come and help!" Every night I had the same nightmare and would wake in a panic. Mum would regularly sit on my bed at 5am and tell me about the milkman who was up and already out of bed on his delivery rounds. In fact, she had a knack for telling stories and is a writer of some talent who has written children's stories and short poems.

Mum's job was being mother to her children and Dad's wife—roles that she made the centre of her life. Nothing was too much bother for Mum, and she would always accommodate my demanding voice. When I came back from school asking for my tea, she would jump to it and provide whatever I needed. Mum waited on us as if we were all her special babies and was completely dedicated to loving us equally. And as if she didn't have enough to do, Mum also cared for everyone else's children like her own.

As well as looking after everyone and writing, Mum worked as a sewing teacher and was also an excellent hairdresser. At the ripe old age of 93, she recently cut my fringe! And I forgot to mention, she was the only mum for miles who made a brilliant curry. In the 1970s in white middle-class suburbia in Chandler's Ford, people didn't know what a curry was until they turned up at the Rossiter household and their mouths were set on fire.

Earning my Place

It took me a while to understand the simple notion that my mum was also my true guardian. When you're adopted, you rarely take things for granted as it's difficult to get your head around the basic fact that your birth is your right. I've always had a feeling that I had to earn my place—that, if I kept behaving, being kind and pleasing, my family would love me and choose to keep me.

Gradually, though, Mum's unconditional love became the foundation on which my strength came to be built. Mum and Dad never criticised me, only tried to give me confidence. They rarely shouted at me. On the few occasions that Mum did so, I quickly listened and retreated. They always saw the best in me. And, let me tell you, I was no angel. In fact, I could be quite naughty. As a teenager, I got caught many times doing things I shouldn't, including a few occasions when boys climbed in my window. I always had an accomplice: my friend Nikki Parker practically lived at my house. We would sleep top and tail in my single bed, with an easy escape route out of my window and into the hedge. Poor Mum and Dad and my brother Ian put up with my tricky ways with utter grace and dignity.

When I told her that I was writing this book, Mum said with a smile, "Oh, Jenny, I'm so looking forward to reading about you." Such interest still in what I'm going to say and do next! I've never met anyone so accepting of who I am, with so little judgment and zero expectation of getting anything back. What I did to deserve my mum I'll never know, but I give thanks every day and feel grateful every second.

"You Can and Will do Anything You Like"

As I write, Mum is 93 and, although quite frail, as strong as an ox. As she and Dad live nearby in Berkshire, I am now able to return a fraction of their love. Truth be known, it quite suits Mum being loved back and waited on a bit as she relaxes in her chair—even though my soup, lemon pudding and cheese, onion and potato pie always come in for a little criticism and she declines with a smile. While it is an honour and privilege to give her all I can, we both know that, however hard I try, I will never be anywhere near as good as her at looking after people. Never as kind and nowhere near as humble. As I say, Mum's life was us. How lucky I am.

Alongside my wonderful mum stood my wonderful dad. They are a couple who are so different yet also so similar. While Mum was a vegetarian and teetotal, Dad loved a drink, a laugh and an adventure. He worked in the advertising section of the local newspaper in Southampton, which was busy and stressful, so sometimes relaxed and stayed out late with his mates, having a laugh and a few drinks.

We didn't mind at home because, when Dad was out, I did what I liked, and when he returned, he would make us all laugh and I would continue to get away with murder. I thought I had my dad wrapped around my little finger, and he allowed me to think that this was true. But really his kindness, encouragement and acceptance gave me everything I needed. Dad taught me many things, but his main point was that I would "always be all right because you're quite all right yourself".

With Dad being so busy at work, he wasn't always that reliable—like the night I was left stranded, aged eight, at Brownies. Dad failed to pick me up, much to the annoyance of a scowling Brown Owl, who rang Mum. Within 30 minutes, she arrived after running non-stop for a mile. Dad got home many hours, and a few drinks, later to inform me, rather jollily: "Jen, this is your one and only lesson. You have learnt that you must never rely on a man." Mum wasn't so amused—or grateful—for his spontaneous life lesson. But this particular one has set me in good stead.

Dad has always seen the best in me, even when I've been bad. I would become a shocking teenager but he, like Mum, never judged. He always found the good in his "little golden girl". Even now, he often says: "You were such a wonderful little girl." He can't even recall the difficulties I caused. Isn't it incredible what a loving memory does? It eradicates all that is unpleasant and replaces it with something far more kind and healing. It was Dad who would say: "Yes, of course you can, Jenny. You can and will do anything you like." He was never worried about me and never doubted my ability, even though I struggled to spell the simplest word and couldn't recite the two times table. He always said: "You get on with people, Jenny, and that is your gift and skill. You will be just fine. You will never have anything to worry about."

Sibling Strife

Mum and Dad were the best parents I could have wished for. But there was one other family member I had to get along with—my brother Ian.

Like any little sister, I admired my big brother and was always trying to get his attention. And like most little sisters, I was generally just an annoyance. He was far more interested in hanging out with his mates than constantly explaining and repeating himself to me.

I was continually asking questions—"How do you spell that?", "What does that mean?"—with no interest in looking at a dictionary, let alone a thesaurus. Ian bought me a dictionary once and stuck a sticker on the back saying *READ ME* in big capital letters. I still have it. And I've rarely opened it.

Regardless of our difficulties and differences, I knew we loved each other from the very beginning. This was never in question. On reflection, it must have been much harder for Ian than it was for me, a new little girl in the family getting all the attention. But Ian made me feel welcome, equal and never an outsider.

So, although we had much to deal with alongside the normal sibling rivalry, we had a strong bond, and as the son of Brian and Jean, he is as deeply loving as they are. He just found it harder to show it. Ian and I have, and always will have, love and respect for each other, but we never waste time on pleasantries. When I call "Ian, I need help!", he comes immediately. Just like Mum used to when I called out "Muuummmmy!" at night. I've had to swallow my pride more than a few times, asking for help with my dissertation or a complex work issue. At the end of the day, my brother Ian is much smarter than me. He's got the brains, leaving me with the limelight of the brawn.

Love—and Rejection

I never knew my mum's mum, Nanny Cole, but I loved my dad's mum, Nanny Rossiter. She brought me cream cakes and sweets every Wednesday, and we played cards for old pennies. She and my grandad lived in a twelfth-floor flat looking out at Weston Shore, Southampton's last remaining shoreline. We would watch the cruise liners and eat crisps and cream soda on the shingle beach. I loved visiting their cosy flat, being spoilt by Nanny and Grandad Rossiter. Again, the love I received from them was endless and always unconditional.

Now, as a parent, I look back and realise that I will never live up to what my parents were to me, and I'm afraid that I will never be the parent they were.

Is it because I was adopted that I got this special treatment? Did they feel they had to try extra hard? Maybe yes, maybe no, but you can't pretend to be a loving parent; you either are or you aren't.

Never was my parents' understanding more greatly needed than in my late teens.

I was still seeking approval and struggling to cope with what is often an intrinsic problem for an adopted child: I had growing feelings of split loyalty. It was difficult in the 1970s, when the closed adoption system would not allow you to be both with your adopted family while allowing you to feel part of your birth family too. It was illegal to have access to any information about my birth family until I was 18. Imagine that as a child—banished from knowing where you came from and any trace of your blood relatives. I felt such shame in even secretly wanting to know and felt like I'd done something wrong by even thinking in this way.

On the one hand, I was grateful to my mum and dad for adopting me, while on the other I was harbouring real feelings of sadness and grief over my birth parents, wondering why they didn't keep me and what I had done that made them not want me. Such feelings of rejection sometimes saw me cry myself to sleep. And, to make matters worse, I couldn't talk about any of it. In those days, these matters were taboo.

Added to which, the rules prevented my birth family from making any approach to my adopted family. And it wasn't really the fact of being adopted that mattered. It was more the lack of understanding, along with wondering why my mother did not want me. All the time I was wrestling with these massive unknowns such as 'How and why do I exist?'. All of this I had to puzzle on my own.

"Adoption loss is the only trauma in the world where the victims are expected by the whole of society to be grateful."
Reverend Keith C Griffith

So, despite a loving home life, my growing maturity saw feelings of rejection increasing, along with wondering about my birth parents. I think that, in some ways, perhaps we all lost in adoption. If only my feelings had been acknowledged, I would have had a very different experience, I am sure.

Going off the Rails

These feelings were starting to show in the outside world. In school, I was displaying signs of personal uncertainties and an underlying anxiety. Reports from Thornden School consistently stated: *Jenny doesn't concentrate*, flagging up the ADHD (attention deficit hyperactivity disorder) which was becoming ever more apparent but would not be officially diagnosed until much later in my life.

Nobody talked about ADHD, although it was obvious that I had issues in the classroom with concentration and comprehension. The problem was that I did not apply myself to subjects I was not interested in. Even today, I cannot absorb material I don't have some kind of connection with. At Thornden, I busied myself by having a laugh with my school friends, hanging around with the wrong crowd and going slightly off the rails.

All the difficulties in the classroom didn't seem important to me as I made up for them with my social life. And at the end of the day, importantly, I wasn't being judged at home. Indeed, through it all, my dad continued to have faith in me, reminding me that "You will be all right because you get on with people".

But my teachers were beginning to lose faith in me. I was really mean to my maths teacher, along with the rest of the class, to the point where she ran out of the classroom in tears. I felt really bad about that at the time and have never really forgiven myself.

Mostly I was mischievous, though, rather than malicious. One day I was caught smoking in the bike sheds by Mr Oakshot. His response? He did a run-up and hit me hard three times on my hand with five rulers stuck together. This was the corporal punishment for girls; the boys got the cane, but they would put a book in their trousers so it didn't hurt as much.

Finding my Direction

But just in the nick of time, I was to redeem myself in the eyes of Thornden (school themes: Aspiration, Respect, Enjoyment, Participation). Aged 14, I came to the realisation that I wanted a career in nursing. With that, I came out of my nosedive. I had to get GCSEs and A levels if I was to fulfil my ambition.

Nursing was always there. I just hadn't realised it until then. Along with the fact that my birth mother was a nurse, I had loved to dress up in a nurse's uniform as a child, playing at caring for patients. I'd also undertaken cleaning work in an old people's home recently, which had given me an insight into the caring profession. I just knew that nursing was for me.

With a new direction and purpose, I sorted out my subject options and concentrated on those that I liked most, knuckling down to work. I was now studying subjects that I enjoyed with teachers I admired. In my final year, I even won the Girl of the Year award and received a silver spoon. And I passed my exams. With seven GCSEs in the bag, at 16 I rejoiced in my profound sense of achievement. My god, I've done it! I thought. I had turned things around.

Continuing this upward trajectory and relentless drive, I went off to Eastleigh technical college and acquired English and maths GCSEs (it took me a few attempts) and two A levels—in psychology and sociology. Where there is a will there is a way.

Armed with these qualifications, I applied to a series of London hospitals and was accepted at St Bartholomew's, the Nightingale and the Whittington—my top three choices. I wanted to live in London, where I was born, and make the break from Chandler's Ford, which was a little too white middle-class suburbia for me. Plus, I needed an adventure.

This was a big moment for me. I had gained nine GCSEs and two A levels and been accepted at three of the best hospitals in London. This seems like small fry to the youngsters of today, but in those days it was nothing short of a miracle. The lost little girl who couldn't stop gazing out of the window ended up with a silver spoon and her first big achievement. This sequence taught me that if I applied myself, I could achieve anything. Equally important after my early rejection: I was wanted not only at home but by the outside world.

I had come from being that little girl who sat at the back of the class feeling stupid and not able to keep up with the basics to an emergent woman, astounded at my achievement. Here I was, beginning a career I had only dreamed of, and my parents could not believe it either.

As I stood ready for the next stage in my life, I pondered that I was born a Ching, was almost an Allen and had ended up a Rossiter. Whoever I was in name, I was about to find out more about myself than I ever expected.

Lessons
1. Love can conquer anything.
2. You have a right to your place.
3. Apply yourself and you can achieve your dreams.

CHAPTER 2

OUT INTO THE WORLD

Finding my Place Outside the Family

Leaving my home in Chandler's Ford, Southampton was not hard for me but would prove a bit traumatic for my mum and dad. On some level, I'd been imagining this day since I was five, when I wore my very first nurse's uniform. Mum was in hospital having an operation, and I visited her in my dress-up nurse's outfit. All the nursing staff loved this, sitting me on their knees before handing me a box of chocolates. Was this the moment the idea of nursing as a career became fixed in my brain? Perhaps. Later it became clearer. And now, aged 18, I had no doubts that this was the path for me.

I would soon be off to London and the big, bright lights—back to the place where I was born—setting off to live out my childhood dream. I had opted for nursing training at St Bartholomew's (Barts) after securing a place in what, to my mind, was the best hospital. It was certainly the oldest in Britain, still providing medical services on its original site. To have gained enough qualifications and work experience to get into Barts was amazing, given that I didn't find school too easy due to my challenging start and my neurodiversity (ADHD).

Early Entrepreneurial Exploits and Cleaning Toilets

Before taking up my place, there were more laughs to be had with three months of fun in the Spanish sun, pursuing one of the great needs of life: earning some cash. The seeds of my entrepreneurial spirit had been sown from the age of 12 as I worked in various part-time jobs and discovered the value of money. I realised from an early age that by working hard and earning money, I could get the things I wanted (clothes and make-up in those days—much the same now). Alongside nurturing my nursing dream, I had, and always will have, some scheme up my sleeve to make sure I was financially independent—even if it meant cleaning toilets.

Cleaning in a nursing home was my first paid job. I chose it because I could chat to the patients as I dusted their rooms. There I gained my first insight into nursing, and I loved it from the start. It was the most natural thing to me; I felt at home being kind to people.

Although I had a few part-time jobs, working in this nursing home was my favourite. Eventually I was promoted from cleaner to auxiliary nurse, and with this new role came my first official nursing uniform—white with a red belt—which I wore with pride. For me, this job offered the perfect mix: friends, money, clothes, make-up and fun. These five elements run right through my story. They are integral to the way I have worked—and lived—and always will be.

After completing my A levels, and before starting my official training at Barts in January 1988, I thought: Right Jen, you've got a good window here. How about a little adventure in the sun before you start? I took a chance and booked a seat on a plane to the Canary Islands. I arrived with no job, but this was all part of the adventure. And it didn't take me long to land a position in a timeshare company, which was the big thing in those days—and where I discovered I could earn some serious money.

Based in Tenerife, the business was a bit of a scam operation really. My task was to scoot around on my moped, chat to potential interested parties and entice them into a taxi bound for our offices, where my colleagues applied the hard sell. For this, I got as much as £450 a week—a lot of money in those days. Through this job, I met two wonderful friends, Sally and Anna, and we all lived in a little flat and shared several months of fun in the winter sun.

Holding Hands, and Curried Goat

By Christmas, my Canaries interlude was over. Time to count my money, put away the suncream and return home to begin my nursing career. On a cold winter's day in January 1988, Mum and Dad drove me to London and to Barts, then a collection of sprawling Victorian buildings in the Smithfield Market area. It was a stressful moment for them. They were very much Southampton people, born and brought up, were not great travellers and certainly never ventured anywhere near the capital. They dropped me off at Barts, more or less threw me out of the car, and shot back home before it got dark.

I stood in my new room, looked out into the square and spotted a girl walking with her mum and dad. Feeling a bit homesick, I began to wish that my mum and dad had stayed with me. But I quickly overcame that wobbly moment as Jo —the girl who had been walking across the square—strolled past my room and we smiled, greeting each other: "Are you starting your nurse training, too?"

Jo immediately became one of my best friends and my partner in crime. Both of us had rooms overlooking the square with the teaching building a short walk away. We were known for our mischievous and raucous ways, but Jo was calming and smart, though always encouraging my hare-brained schemes.

Nurses took a real pride in their uniforms. You were expected to wear them correctly, as was made clear at the Preliminary Training School. Strict discipline was enforced on this, and nail varnish, wristwatches and jewellery were all banned. Mind you, this didn't stop us until we got a stern telling off.

We wore a beautiful, blue-check, old-fashioned uniform which, along with a dress and an apron, included a hat formed of material we had to shape over a cake tin and then fold in a special way. This uniform was much better than the one that I'd dreamt of when I was five, and Jo was a dab hand at making the best nursing crown of all.

When you qualified, you wore a dark-blue belt with a special buckle which you had to buy yourself. Mine was an antique silver one with cherubs on it that I still have. As you progressed from years one, two and three, you had different coloured belts (with no special buckle) and the hospital sisters wore tall, starched hats. We had to refer to them by their ward name, such as Sister Percival Potts.

It was all so friendly: corridors full of girls all getting along and sharing facilities. I really felt at home, and my three years there would turn out to be some of the best yet. More than that, London offered something very different from my previous life. It was all so new and exciting for me and I felt immediately at home. The white, middle-class environment I'd been brought up in I felt was a little limited for me. Now I was experiencing so much more—mixing with different people, nationalities and religions, and being exposed to many cultures. I was in my element making friends, socialising and looking after people at their most vulnerable. All this satisfied a great need in me: an endless curiosity to understand the different peoples of the world.

This cultural element to my new life was particularly strong in Barts' sister hospital, the Homerton in Hackney. I loved working there and felt very at home. We jumped on a bus from Barts in the city into East London. During my stint in A&E there, I saw some harrowing sights, from gunshot wounds to stabbings, and while I don't claim to have saved many lives, I always held hands and cared for every single patient.

Through the friends I made, and hands I held, I also shared food. I was introduced to curried goat and sweet fried plantains. I couldn't believe it at first: What, you eat goat? And hot banana? I'd only eaten it cold. I loved my introduction to West Indian food, and curried goat is still my favourite dish of all time although, to my dismay, while enjoying a recent order from my local Caribbean takeaway, the bone took half of my tooth away. And there was my very first crown!

At 22, I qualified as a Registered General Nurse (RGN) with a diploma. I was living the dream, and nursing was turning out to be everything that I hoped it would be— the pay apart, which never bothered me anyway as I knew I could always make extra money. From there, I chose to work in a surgical ward at the Homerton hospital, where I felt most at home.

This meant Jo and me moving flats, first to Leytonstone and then to hospital accommodation in Hoxton Street, which was fantastic. We lived next to a jellied eel shop. I never did taste the jellied eels and mash with green liquor to soak it all up. That was just taking the whole thing too far for me, and I am proud to say, I haven't tried it to this day. But we often went into the Hoxton pubs and danced on the tables and sang karaoke with the locals. I returned there recently and, although it's completely different and pretty fancy now, I am sure I saw a few of the same people that we were dancing and singing with 30 years earlier.

Specialising: Psychiatric Nursing

Even though I revelled in this whole nursing and London scene, I was having to give some thought to what I wanted to do next. I loved being a general nurse but realised that it was people's hearts and minds that I was most interested in, rather than treating physical illness or injury. I was ready to make my next move and continue my path in psychiatry and psychology. As an RGN with a diploma, I was quickly accepted on to an 18-month degree course at Bournemouth University in clinical psychiatry and nursing. This offered the chance to graduate with a nursing degree and qualify as a psychiatric nurse, which was the next step in carving out my path.

Off then to sunny Bournemouth in 1993, where I lived happily for four years. Unfortunately, nursing there was very different from London, and the mental health system in the town was somewhat Dickensian. The use of sedation and electric-shock treatment was desperately sad and sickened me. This wasn't what I knew and wanted to be a part of. I decided then that I did not want to be a nurse in a hospital where there was no prospect of making the changes that I was so desperate to see. People at their most vulnerable and weak needed to be treated with respect, not forced to take treatment they were not well enough to consent to.

A New Work Family: Pharmaceuticals

Where would the Jenny journey take me next? I had a degree and loved being a nurse, yet part of me was frustrated. Although I could help fix the person, I couldn't influence the system. I wanted to bring about change and felt completely frustrated that I could not make the obvious positive shifts in care in these hospitals. This is a theme I have noticed in my life: you can change yourself, help others do the same, but it is naive to think that you can change the system. You can challenge the system but changing it overnight? Not a chance. At least not single-handedly anyway. With my frustrations at the intractability of the system, I continued my search.

Maybe there were other areas of health care to explore and perhaps, regrettably, front line nursing was not the place for me after all. With my drive for change allied to my entrepreneurial instincts, I was about to discover my second work family—the pharmaceutical industry. This world fascinated me. I loved the science and innovation that enabled products to be made which cured people and even saved lives. As a nurse, I'd seen the effects of novel medicines first-hand. Moving into this space was a good match and meant I didn't have to leave my first work family, the NHS.

Once I'd decided on this new direction, after some research, I applied for a job as a rep in the pharmaceutical division of Procter & Gamble (P&G), which was founded in 1837 by brothers-in-law William Procter, a candle maker, and James Gamble, a soap maker. These products became the foundation of their business.

The company attracts some of the finest talent in the world and enjoys a first-class global reputation for its marketing in particular. And once you are part of the P&G family, you are treated as one of its own. It is a company that values performance and diversity, operates a policy of promoting and rewarding from within, and acknowledges that people are its biggest asset. This was a company I wanted to be a part of.

So, I applied for the job and was offered an interview. But it proved harder to get in than I had expected, with lots of capability and reasoning tests, which unfortunately didn't sit well with my neurodiversity. Despite a good interview with a lovable, slightly-madcap character called Alan Potter, I left despondent, believing that my cognitive ability might have just let me down.

When the phone rang, to my utter surprise the recruiter said, "Congratulations, you have passed the recruitment process and you have the job." I could not believe my luck. I dropped my coffee and literally fell of my chair. The truth be known, I'm sure I didn't pass the tests. But Alan Potter liked me. He knew that I would be good at the job, which was all that mattered. I was in, and my tests results must have been thrown in the bin.

I was soon out on the road, in October 1993, as a territory manager for Dorset and Wiltshire. It was the beginning of a wonderful career, new relationships and many achievements. I soon became successful, as the role really suited me. I spent all my working hours serving and educating my NHS customers on P&G's innovative products, including the very first bisphosphonate—a type of drug that prevents the loss of bone density—for osteoporosis. In the process, I met consultants, GPs and nurses—and, of course, many became great friends.

What I loved about this job was this: I was with 'my people', doctors and nurses who spoke the same language and shared a common purpose. We might have worked for different organisations, but we knew that it was the patients who mattered the most. As a pharmaceutical rep, I wasn't working directly with patients—and, I'm not going to lie, I really did miss that—but still, I was on the same wavelength as the medical professionals. I didn't have to persuade or sell, just have a human conversation about what's best for patients. It really was that simple.

Once, a senior marketing guy came to find out why I was so successful. For all his fancy marketing qualifications, he didn't have the first clue about what it took just to get on with people—to be yourself and genuinely care. He just didn't understand this basic skill of human connection. Instead, he made a sexist assumption and left: "I know how you do it: you charm all the men." In those days it was acceptable to say something like that. I am pleased to say that in the main the P&G ethos was not in line with his, and I loved my work family for that.

Within 18 months, I started training and coaching others and won the P&G president's award for the top European performance.

My P&G training was second to none, and I am so grateful as it provided the foundations for my commercial and business acumen. I was lucky to get this job, and I will never forget the people at P&G for taking a punt on me and seeing the potential beyond the tests. Then again, I think that they were also lucky to have me.

After a few years of achievement and satisfaction in the pharmaceutical division, I fancied exploring another division and expanding my market experience. The first step proved to be an internal switch to managing an area of P&G's fragrance division. This proved a short-lived move and taught me that the retail division was not for me. I learnt then that, although I liked the commercial side of life, without purpose and meaning the journey is not worth the money alone. This was another important lesson in life.

By switching divisions and making a wrong move, this gave me the chance to take stock. I needed a fresh career challenge and to move my life on. I had the necessary incentive to broaden my horizons and take the next plunge of my life: leaving P&G and setting sail for New Zealand.

Lessons
1. You can't change the system overnight.
2. Money is worth nothing without meaning and purpose.
3. A wrong move is often the necessary incentive to make the right move.

CHAPTER 3

LORRAINE, PETER AND NEDDY

Meeting my Birth Family

Even as my career had been going full pelt, thoughts about my birth parents were never far away. My voyage of discovery with them began in 1990 when, aged 21, I was entitled to find out about my biological family by law and uncovered the full details about Lorraine. I went to St Catherine's House in London to investigate the circumstances of my birth and, after some lengthy detective work, I tracked her down. Through friends, I made contact by letter, to which I got this reply:

> *Dear Jenny Elizabeth, nobody knows about you and I would like to keep it that way. I wish you every success in your future life. Thank you for writing, Lorraine.*

It was like a blow to my stomach. Hope had been replaced by more rejection. And I assumed this was the end of things with Lorraine. I tried to put thoughts of my birth mother out of my mind. I would never have any kind of relationship with her, and I would have to accept that.

But, nine years later, completely out of the blue, she re-engaged:

Dear Jenny Elizabeth
I am visiting the UK in December and would be able to meet with you if you are still interested in this.
My circumstances have changed and I am now able to meet or correspond with you… I have two children, Gemma and Benson, who know of you and will be in the UK with me and would like to meet with you…

Like Looking in a Mirror

On Boxing Day 1996 I set eyes on my birth mother and my half-siblings for the first time. It was an emotional moment, indescribable to someone who's never been through it. Looking at my birth mother for the very first time and clapping eyes on someone who looked just like me was simultaneously one of the oddest and most normalising experiences I've ever had.

When you are surrounded by people who look like you, you probably never even give it a second thought. For me, growing up with no blood relatives, this was an experience I'd never had. When I first saw my birth mother, it was like I was looking in a mirror.

Adopted children are often trying to make sense of an environment where they don't quite belong or, indeed, don't even come from. Without that solid foundation of knowing where you're from, it can be pretty shaky ground. It is a world where you've never seen anyone who looks vaguely like you, and you can't begin to imagine what your blood relatives—your original tribe—might have been like. Genetics is strange like that.

My first meeting with Lorraine and her children was in Islington, where they were staying in a rented apartment. I had longed for this moment for as long as I could remember. I was desperately excited.

To meet my birth mother was an extraordinary moment, yet it also seemed like the most natural thing in the world. Lorraine was alone, as Gemma and Benson had gone out. I knew what to expect visually as by then I had photos of her as a young woman. But seeing her in the flesh was indescribably wonderful for an adopted child craving to connect with, and relate to, her family. I couldn't stop looking at my birth mother and hung on to her every word.

Lorraine was quite regal in her stance. She had a look in her eyes and a smile that reflected my own. Immediately, I knew she took no nonsense, and there would be no messing from me. She laughed like me, and I soon found out that her abysmal sense of direction and spelling were traits that she had passed on. She told me that when she walked out of a hotel, it was extremely difficult for her to find her way back. My muddled head, and how I would walk up the street in the wrong direction, had always been something I was ashamed about. Knowing that this was a shared experience with Lorraine made me feel a whole lot better about myself.

Wow! I thought. I'm just like you!

"Oh, Jenny, You Took Your Time!"

When Gemma and Benson returned, we celebrated our getting together well into the night. We continued to meet for the rest of their two-week (and what turned out to be only) visit to the UK, which included taking Lorraine to meet my parents in Southampton.

As we passed my old school, she remarked: "Jenny, I really wanted you to be brought up in a family that was solid and safe. And I am so happy to meet your parents and see that you've had the life I wished for you."

We then drove on to visit Peter in his tiny flat at 6 Cecil Court, Castle Street, Wimborne. Oh, yes, not only had I found my birth mother and my half siblings, but a few years earlier, I'd found my biological father too.

Peter was very different from Lorraine. For a start, he had wanted me from the outset. It meant that my relationship with him, though it would turn out to be brief, was loving and truly special.

I had been searching for Peter with no success up to the time I was based in Bournemouth doing my degree in the early 1990s. While on that course, I was nursing part-time at a hospital in Southampton to earn some money to fund my degree. One day, I was talking to a patient named Steve and told him about the hunt for my birth father. I gave him the scant information I had about Peter and, despite my scepticism, he said, confidently: "I will find him. Leave it with me."The next thing I knew, Steve dropped me this note:

Dear Jenny

We look to begin our investigations by your answering this simple questionnaire which shall, at least, arm us with the basic criteria for which we hope will prove a very satisfactory end … do not worry about answering them all… we shall also need the analysis of all the adoption details. However, due to your individual circumstances, they might not be relevant as your father's details are not always noted or, indeed, necessary.

Having gathered all the information that I could from the adoption records, I passed it on to Steve.

To my complete astonishment, within 48 hours Steve rang me to say that he had found Peter and had come up with his full contact details. He had spoken to my birth father, who was now living in a cottage in the town of Cullompton in Devon, and Peter was keen for me to make contact. I have no idea how Steve did this. Perhaps it was Peter's coin-dealer public profile? Whatever it was, he had employed quick detective work.

Inevitably, I had always wondered and worried about Peter. What was he like? How would he react to me? So, it was with a mixture of excitement and trepidation that I took my courage in my hands and phoned him from an old red public call box in Southbourne, where I lived.

The ringtone seemed to go on forever. Finally a man answered. He had a gruff, cigar smoke, red-wine-stained voice: "Hello."

"Hi, it's Jenny here," I could only think to reply.

"Oh, Jenny," he came back, "you took your time! When are you coming to see me?"

With this, we agreed I would visit Peter the following weekend, and he said: "I'll send my driver." (Oh my god, he has got his own driver!) His personal 'driver' turned out to be a taxi driver he used. Peter was a man about town and always took taxis. Anyway, it was grand gesture on his part and typical of him.

The taxi came all the way from the deep dark countryside of Cullompton to pick me up in Southbourne and took me back to Peter's place at Lanes Cottage, which proved to be a real Hansel and Gretel affair, to be found through woods and set remotely down a country lane. It was a magical setting for what would become a magical relationship.

I was nervous about that first meeting and kept thinking: What on earth am I doing? The brave adventurer was again having doubts. But Peter was there to greet me, standing by the gate and smiling. He had black teeth and such dark-olive skin and eyes that I wondered how he could possibly be my birth father. I was about to be spending the next 48 hours in the middle of nowhere with what was, after all, a complete stranger. Was this another fine mess I had got myself into?

But, like me at that time, Peter drank red wine and smoked like a trooper—and we got along like a house on fire. So we spent the whole weekend in a cosy sitting room heated by a wood fire, telling tales, smoking, imbibing wine and eating wonderful food that Peter had cooked. He had set me up in a little bedroom with fresh flowers in a vase and a bed with a patchwork quilt.

The relationship continued as it began that first weekend. I followed Peter around on his adventures, and we sampled the local wines—"It doesn't matter how good or bad the wine is. After the first glass it all tastes good!" As well as the wine, Peter enjoyed cooking exotic food from all over the globe. And, often over a meal, we would talk late into the night about what I should do with my life. All the while, I was absorbing Peter's wisdom and knowledge whatever the subject, be it fear, money or boyfriends. At the time, I didn't realise how useful this would be throughout my life.

Peter later moved to France for a year (with more wine drinking, of course) and then he moved to Wimborne to be near me for his final years and where, as mentioned, he met up with Lorraine on her UK visit. Peter was an incredibly kind and generous man and treated me like a princess, giving me so much of what he didn't have, as his grandmother had done for him.

I had assumed that Peter must be rich. In fact, he had very little money by the time I met him. In his working life, he had made a lot of money, but he had largely burned through it all. To keep going, he had sold the Cullompton cottage, rented it back and lived on the absolute basics (leaving me with an £8 BT bill to pay when he died).

We fell out just once over the nine years that I knew Peter, and it was over my career choices. He disagreed with my quitting my P&G job in New Zealand (where I was working by then) to do other things.

Peter had lived in such style—a life so full of adventures and entrepreneurship, but he wanted me to have the security of the corporate lifestyle, giving me the means to have more reliable comfort. He need not have worried as, like him, I would find my way through, taking risks, never choosing the obvious path.

The funny thing is that I used to call him Pops, never Dad. I had my one-and-only Dad, and I loved him more than the world. Peter always felt more like Pops—someone who was a good companion, an old and wise soulmate, old enough to be my grandad, in fact. My daughter Poppy is known as Pops now, and if I think about it, she's got a few traits of the wise old soulmate, too.

Peter and I spent our final time together when he moved to Cecil Court, Cranborne in Dorset, by which time he was living a more and more withdrawn life, with a lot of illness in his final few years. He died aged 76 in August 2001, owing that £8 to BT but as a happy man having found me.

Peter's first words to me had been: "You took your time." His last, from his hospital bed, were: "Enjoy yourself and have fun."

This summed him up, and his lasting legacy to me is the traits we shared: bravery, a sense of adventure, a zest for life and an entrepreneurial spirit. Peter believed life was for living, and I do too.

Being an atheist, Peter didn't want a funeral but to be "thrown in a rubbish bin". When I went with my then boyfriend Steve to scatter his ashes in Richmond Park, unbeknown to me at the time there were some left in the urn, which Steve tipped into a bin. When I was later told of this, I thought: that man always got his way in the end!

The trouble with having a birth father and being adopted is that you never know in your heart of hearts if he's the real deal or not. In fact, something that my half-brother Benson later said suggested that Peter might not have been my birth father after all. I will never know for sure (unless, of course, I decide to find out through DNA searching— apparently quite easy these days). But Peter and I shared so many similar traits that, even if he wasn't my real father, I'd met a good match.

He was definitely my second soul father, even if we weren't blood related.

An Unexpected Friendship

One surprising aspect to come out of all of this was my connection with Peter's wife, Irene 'Neddy' Allen.

Peter used to say to me that when he died, Neddy and I would be friends—and that turned out to be true. When Peter was alive, Neddy did not want to speak to, nor have anything to do with me, and I cannot blame her for that. I was the child who effectively broke her marriage, after all.

Her stance changed when I made the arrangements for Peter's funeral. From there on, we talked on the phone, and I would visit her in her flat in Dorset Square, their marital home, which Peter had bought in the early 1960s.

Although in later years Neddy became blind and her health went downhill, we kept up to date. My relationship with her had great meaning for me. She was like Peter in so many ways; it often felt like I was still speaking to him. I took boyfriends, my ex-husband and Poppy to meet her, and I helped her to communicate with clients, as well as doing odd jobs for her.

As a mark of our established friendship, about five years ago Neddy passed on to me a wonderful lucky-horseshoe brooch that had belonged to Peter's Spanish grandmother from Andalusia. As described in Chapter 1, caring for him so much, this poverty-stricken woman ate the banana skins so that Peter could have the fruit. This selflessness and generosity of spirit was passed on to Peter.

It transpires that Peter's grandmother had worn that brooch every day, and he had wanted me to have it after he died. It is one of the most meaningful objects that I possess as it represents the luck I have been bestowed with despite the difficulties.

Then for a while, in 2020, I tried calling Neddy a few times over the spring and summer with no answer.

When I emailed her also and had no response, I thought she must have gone to stay with her nieces due to the pandemic. Neddy was needing more care as she had been quite unwell and was not coping in her flat. I assumed that she had turned to her nieces for help—they were part of her large Italian family, which I never met as she kept me totally separate from them. I continued to search for information about her only to discover, via the Internet, that she had died.

I was really sad to hear this and upset that nobody had thought to inform me.

Split Loyalties: a Challenge for an Adopted Child

The initial excitement of the UK meeting with Lorraine, Gemma and Benson was as good as it got, really. Lorraine, I feel, reached out and met me more than halfway emotionally. But, as with many emotional tales, ultimately things went a bit wonky.

As I mentioned, on that first visit Lorraine and I visited Peter in his tiny flat in Dorset. An unforgettable and emotional occasion for two reasons: it was the first and only time I would see my birth parents together and almost certainly the only time they had met since splitting up in 1969.

At one point during that Dorset get-together, Peter sent me out to post a letter, allowing them a few moments to themselves. One can only imagine what was said, and not said. I wish I had been a fly on the wall.

The first meeting with Lorraine was the catalyst for a monumental decision. Having connected with my new/old family, and at a time when my career at P&G appeared to have hit the buffers, the thought of moving to New Zealand and to a new challenge proved irresistible, and I linked up with them there (detailed in Chapter 4).

My relationship with Lorraine and her children has taken a few turns. For many years after my move to New Zealand, we went our separate ways.

But after much reflection and tentative attempts at reconnection, Gemma, Benson and I are back in touch. Since the start of the Covid-19 pandemic, in March 2020, we have shared what have sometimes been emotional connections online. This has been one of the many positives to come out of the pandemic, and I am really happy to be back in contact with my half siblings. Both are now in their forties and have children of their own.

As far as Gemma is concerned, I sense that from the outset she was upset to discover my existence as she had assumed that she was Lorraine's eldest child. It must have been awful later in life to realise that she had an older half-sister she knew nothing about. It must have thrown up many difficult emotions. But the fact remains that we are all part of a family puzzle, although sadly Lorraine will now not talk about it. Once Lorraine has made a decision, that is it—nothing can soften her iron-like conviction and resolve. Funnily enough, my partner David recently said the same about me!

We have had many laughs along with the tears, though. And, I suppose, with the good times mixed with the bad, we were just like any other family. Over the years, as part of my profession, I have studied the dynamics of family life and, through my training and understanding, I know that the adoption dynamic is a difficult and complicated one to manage. Having two family systems is tricky as you have to deal with a level of split loyalty. It is, after all, a cleft that is unnatural and goes against our true nature. As social animals, we need to feel safe in our tribe. Belonging in that tribe is all we need to thrive.

I've come full circle with all of this. For some parts of it, I was sad and felt rejected. But this wasn't true rejection as Lorraine allowed me to exist. After much reflection, I realise that the greatest gift that I was given was the gift of life.

And, for that brave move by a 24-year-old woman, away from her home and in the middle of London, I am eternally grateful. She gave me a life, even though choosing to live her life without me. I went on to have a family and a home. It was just not with her.

These were my experiences with Lorraine and her children, and with Peter and Neddy, to go with the times that I have shared with my adoptive parents, Brian and Jean. My three families.

Your birth parents may create you, but it is you who chooses who you are and, in my case, I have learnt so much from the three families I have been a part of—which I will detail later on. They are life lessons which have set a course for me and have made me the person I am.

Lessons

1. Don't feel ashamed of things that you cannot change.
2. Life is for living: enjoy yourself and have fun.
3. Look at rejection differently, and you may realise it's not really rejection at all.

CHAPTER 4

NEW ZEALAND, A NEW BUSINESS AND A NEW LIFE

Learning How to Grow

Not long after my first meeting with Lorraine, I felt that I had done all I could professionally at P&G for the time being and was ready for another adventure. I had learnt much in pharmaceuticals, my favourite company division, but realised that I needed a new challenge. It was 1997.

Through my birth mother, I was granted New Zealand citizenship immediately and, with it, a full passport. With this in hand, I resigned from P&G, only for the company to offer me a post in its New Zealand grocery division. Before I knew it, I was on my travels again.

With all my belongings in two big boxes already in transit, I turned up at Heathrow and waved goodbye to my mum, dad, brother Ian and boyfriend Matt. I walked through the passport barrier with a little glance back. Then a large smile took over my face. I was setting off on another big adventure. This time, to the other side of the world.

A Sharp Change of Heart

When I arrived in New Zealand, I was beyond excited. My half-sister Gemma warmly welcomed me at Auckland Airport, and I was filled with all the hopes in the world. Sadly, this welcome did not extend much further than a few days.

Although I'm not sure what I really expected, I never in a million years anticipated this.

Things went downhill quickly, both on the personal and work front. What seemed like just 48 hours after my arrival, Gemma decided that she no longer wanted anything to do with me

Maybe I said the wrong things, maybe my very presence was too intense, but I think the reality of me just being me, a new half-sister turning up in her homeland, was too much for her. Or perhaps I'm just a horrible person! Whatever was behind it, my half-sister had a sharp change of heart. This was a sad and upsetting time for me, but at the end of the day, this relationship was just not meant to be.

Gemma grew up thinking she was the eldest girl. My arrival was dropped like a bombshell, and at the time I couldn't see her perspective or the impact it had. Through my adopted-child eyes, Pollyanna style, I thought that all would be rosy in my fantasy family. In walks Twinkletoes, the big sister, thinking she has the right to her place and even her friends. Well, it just doesn't work like that, and Gemma told me where to go and booted me out of sight. I just was not welcome, regardless of my place.

It wasn't just Gemma who didn't want anything to do with me, though. Neither did Lorraine, and from that point on, I was on my own.

A Change of Plan

Adding to my woes was the fact that I really didn't like my job on the North Island working in the grocery division of P&G, negotiating with small-town supermarket owners.

How I missed the medical world and my absorbing conversations with doctors and nurses, and caring for patients rather than negotiating the cost of washing powder. As I was driving through the rugged mountain ranges beyond Wellington Harbour, a thought suddenly hit me: I could be a nurse again.

With that, my mind was made up. I resigned and took the training required to practise as a psychiatric nurse in a secure psychiatric unit in Wellington Hospital. And this was the start of another fun and incredible adventure and one of the best jobs I've ever had.

Again, I loved my work, my colleagues and that I was in a position to look after and care for some terribly unwell and vulnerable people. I worked nights and rested in the days and started saving for a big trip around New Zealand and then Southeast Asia.

Diving for Pipis, Tramping for Miles, Seeing Stars

Although my birth mother and sister rejected me, in New Zealand I made a whole new family of friends who were kind and welcomed me as their own. Maybe they saw me as the uptight Pommie girl who needed some serious training to become her true, chilled Kiwi self again, but whatever it was, I had some brilliant mates.

My great friend Shellee was my partner in crime. She adopted me as her sister on the very night that Gemma declared her rejection and from that point on spent every weekend with me. Shellee was fun, full of laughter and liked the boys, just like me. When we looked at each other, we knew exactly what the other was thinking. And that was often pure mischief.

I loved the Kiwi lifestyle. We walked for miles at the weekends in the Remutakas and Tararuas mountain ranges (or 'tramping' as they call it) and ate and drank the local food and wine that had been sourced straight from the vineyard or farm. I had been a vegetarian for ten years in the UK, but as soon as I arrived in New Zealand, I became a carnivore again.

I also had a wonderful and sparky friend called Tanya. She was a smart farm girl training to be a doctor. We would go on wild adventures and hang out on her parents' farm, and she kicked me into touch regularly. She had no qualms about telling me how a true Kiwi girl should behave and to stop being so uptight. Tanya didn't care what people thought, and she lived her life just as she liked. She and I would go diving for pipis (*paphies australis*)—delicious shellfish—cook them on the fire and eat them with a few bottles of local wine. We would drive for miles through the Bay of Islands and sleep wherever we liked. On a clear night we would stargaze, and I could never get over the spectacular delight of the stars in the southern hemisphere. They are so much better and brighter than from our rather shady northern perspective with all its light pollution.

The Call of Home

Meanwhile, my bad habit of attracting the wrong men followed me to New Zealand in the shape of Matt, my doctor boyfriend from the UK. Regrettably, I allowed him to join me despite my intuition telling me to do the contrary.

Matt had all the power of charm and charisma to manipulate me. It took me a while to work out that the man who constantly cheated on me with all the nurses back home was doing so again—just in a different a hospital in a different country.

I was furious with myself for wasting time thinking I could change him, or he could change himself. I may be slow to act, but when I do it's final: I grabbed all Matt's clothes and threw them out of our Wellington flat on to the lawn outside, forever shutting the door on his part in my life.

Soon after this, Sarah Pidgley, one of my oldest and closest friends from the UK, and her husband Andy, flew to see me in New Zealand. We travelled to the South Island, where my ancestors were from, and had the best time of our lives. We swam with dolphins, visited the beauty spot of Milford Sound, climbed mountains and skied down them, all the time driving around in Tanya's car singing eighties' songs at the tops of our voices.

This trip was typical of my time in New Zealand, where I was among friends in a place I loved. I felt at home there almost from the moment I landed. I adored the New Zealand countryside with its enormous contrasts—from the tropical parts of the North Island to the mountains and lakes on the South Island. Then there's the openness of the people, who were so welcoming, inviting me into their homes. The country that I was then able to call my home has a fantastic vibe that cannot be equalled.

But although I felt so much like a Kiwi girl, and was having the time of my life, I knew that the Pommie in me was beckoning and calling me back. And I recognised that, at the end of the day, I'm a Londoner, and I needed to go home to my mum and dad.

With my time almost up, I had one final big trip planned before I returned to Blighty. On my way home, I spent three months travelling in Southeast Asia. I arrived in Thailand and travelled by bus to Laos, Vietnam and Cambodia. The bus toppled over at one point and ended up on its side in a rice paddy in the middle of the night.

This trip offered so many new experiences. I even went as far as sampling a dish made of insects on my basic £5-a-day budget. This had to cover all accommodation, which was often in a flea-infested bunk room where I hid my valuables under my pillow at night. There was no five-star hotel for me. I was lucky if I could afford a room with a fan!

The next stop was New Delhi in India, where I met with Ashley, my friend Jo Baruah's brother. Together we spent three long months travelling around the northern part of the country. From the Golden Temple of Amritsar to the burning bodies at Varanasi, this trip was like no other. I fell in love with India the minute I stepped off the plane and the heat hit my face; I decided very quickly that this was my kind of place.

Ashley and I were invited to stay with the beautiful Baruah family in Assam. We travelled in air-conditioned cars, touring the hills of the Assamese tea plantations, and were treated like visiting kings and queens. This was hardly surprising really, as Barua (also spelt Baruah) is a common Assamese surname which is also termed as Rajbansi, meaning 'of royal descent'.

The women of the family would serve us Indian cuisine well into the night, singing, "More rice Jenny? More rice?" We would eat with our right hand only (in India the left hand is for wiping your bottom, cleaning your feet and other unsavoury functions) and the beautiful Baruah queens would never start their food until our plates were overspilling. I was so welcomed and looked after and yet again found a family who treated me as their own. The only downside was that I was the only person ever who came back from India and needed to go on a diet!

To end our trip, we pulled on our hiking boots, hired a guide and trekked the Ghorepani Poon Hill Trek in Nepal.

I spent my final magical month walking the Himalayan hills before getting on a plane to the rain at Heathrow.

Arriving home felt weird after almost three years away. I flew into the UK and thought: This country is so cute. It looks like the back of a chocolate box. The first thing my mum said to me was, "Jenny, you have changed so much!" And she was right. Being away from the UK, I had discovered a new and confident self. The question now was: what would she do next?

Jumping off a Cliff:
Starting a Business

Well, basically I carried on where I had left off. Ashley and I decided to share a flat, renting a tiny place on Camden Road near to Holloway Prison. We had zero cash so had to make do with the little space we had. I had the noisy front room, which I converted with an Ikea bed into a bedroom, and Ashley took the quiet room at the back. We tossed for that, and he won.

I got a job working nights as an agency psychiatric nurse while Ashley found a job in the A&E department at the Royal Free Hospital, where he is now a charge nurse. Together we had great fun as we started enjoying London life again.

But, as luck would have it, one day the phone rang. It was one of my colleagues from P&G, who offered me the chance to return to my P&G of old—pharmaceuticals, my loyal work family. I decided to take the job and move back into the world of business—and of working all hours.

By then I had moved in with my then boyfriend Steve in Molesey near Hampton Court, and I was looking ahead in career terms. While working for P&G offered little time for much else (you put in 13 hours a day there), I gained some brilliant experience in leadership development and gold-standard coaching methods, and trained as a master practitioner in neuro-linguistic programming (NLP) in my spare time. (NLP is an alternative therapy intended to improve self-awareness and change patterns of mental and emotional behaviour.) I might have been back in the world of business, but my passion for people was brighter than ever.

While I was grateful for this further corporate spell at P&G, after two years, my entrepreneurial spirit was becoming restless. So, aged 32, I decided to take the plunge and start my own business. My P&G bosses thought I was mad, but I thought differently.

Let me be clear: I had no pre-existing customers or network to pull on and no redundancy package or lifetime savings to fall back on. I had a mortgage to pay, and by then Steve and I had split up, so I was on my own with no financial security or loving partner to help.

Despite all of this, in October 2002 Inspired Results was born, a coaching and training consultancy for managers and their teams in the pharmaceutical industry. From the outset my business offered a difference: I combined gold-standard coaching with development training, using my experience in psychiatry and psychology as well as my NLP training.

I won my first client quickly, but this contract was not enough to pay the bills. My first year of business was hard graft, nerve-wracking and involved very little sleep. I worked shifts as a psychiatric nurse by night and ran my business by day. Liam the lodger moved into my spare room, while I did everything I could to get my business off the ground. I was so tired that I'd sleep in the bath curled up in a towel on my break during my nursing shifts. One day, I fell asleep in the chair and at 4am in the morning I woke with a start as a very unwell patient was attempting to get into the drug cupboard!

I might have been tired, but I was inspired by my new business—and I was beginning to get results. Anyone who has run their own business knows the lengths you have to go to to make things work. And, as it turned out, that first year was just a taster of the roller coaster that was to come.

Looking for Love

Until now, adventure, career and boyfriends were the order of the day, and marriage was not top of my agenda. However, at a routine surgery consultation, my doctor pointed out that I shouldn't leave having children too much longer. I took this message to heart, and the hunt was on for a husband. Being who I am, and being short of time, I went down the adventurous route and looked for a mate via a speed-dating event in London. This also appealed to my overzealous and mischievous nature—essential ingredients in my character.

Enter Tony, a charming and attractive man who would play an important part in my life. With speed dating, you tick yes to those people you wish to follow up. Feeling that I had ticked yes to too many men, I inexplicably crossed Tony off my list. But the following day, the event organisers told me that he had been in touch with them and wanted to see me again. Taking a chance, I agreed for him to receive my email address—and the rest, as they say, is history.

Tony swept me off my feet. I fell for his great charm and romantic ways—we enjoyed a roast dinner from the boot of his fancy car and talked all night on our mobiles, him keeping me company during my nursing night shifts. Before I knew it, Tony had bought me a car, and I had moved in with him. My new home was a beautiful cottage at Coldharbour near Dorking, where I also fell in love with his two dogs, Bismarck and Phoebe. Tony soon proposed, and we married in Grittleton House in Wiltshire on 27 August 2004.

In the midst of the romance I became pregnant, although it was full of drama as I didn't realise I was expecting. Quite simply, it was the last thing on my mind while I enjoyed the romance of a new and thriving relationship. Then one day, driving round the M25, I developed excruciating stomach pain, the worst I've had in my life.

Somehow, I managed to make it to my GP's surgery.

I had to lie on the floor of the waiting room, the pain was so bad. The medics quickly got me 'blue lighted' to hospital, where the crash team of medics (brought in when things are not looking good) stood over me. It was an ectopic pregnancy, which can be fatal. I was lucky to be saved. Sadly, my baby was not.

As a result, I was left with one fallopian tube, and my chances of getting pregnant again dropped dramatically. Not one to be put off, and relieved that I'd survived, with hope in my heart I picked myself up and tried again, but two years on nothing had happened. I was then referred to an infertility specialist who, on 16 July 2006, reported that the best chance of conception would be IVF.

Loss and Hope

I was devastated. I sobbed and cried for days. My hope for a family seemed lost. Giving birth to a child is such a natural thing and an expectation for most women. Not being able to have your own baby, then, is one of the greatest losses a woman can feel. Being unable to have a child naturally was a massive blow for me. After weeks of utter despair, I managed to pick myself up, and Tony and I decided to give fertility treatment a go.

Then a strange thing happened. After a relaxing holiday in Portugal, and just before I started IVF treatment, I missed my period. I thought I'd better take a pregnancy test just in case and, miraculously, that was the beginning of the life of our Poppy Hope. From that moment, I was the happiest I'd ever been. I loved every minute of my pregnancy: the sickness, the weight gain, the tiredness and the sleepless nights. I went from 9 stone to 13-and-a-half, I was enjoying my pregnancy so much! I didn't know that my baby was a girl but secretly hoped that it was. I talked to my bump every day, and there was never a moment that I didn't feel closely connected to the new life inside me.

Poppy Hope was born in the early hours of 12 July 2007, and I couldn't believe it. The little girl I'd always dreamt of, healthy and alert—the cutest thing I'd ever seen.

The next few years were not so happy as my dream of a big family was dashed. I had four more pregnancies and lost them all. All my little babies who would have joined us to make one big family tribe. Again, more loss that we are not supposed to talk about—just like the loss experienced with adoption.

There was a moment that compounded this for me as I was referred to a miscarriage specialist at St Mary's Hospital, Paddington and found myself walking the corridors of the place where I was born and given away. I was in this place for the second time in my life: the first when my mother didn't want to keep her baby; now as a mother who so desperately wanted more children and couldn't keep them.

Losing these babies produced another profound sense of loss in me and put a further strain on my marriage to Tony. Indeed, after a few good yet rocky years, regrettably in 2010 Tony and I split up and I moved, with three-year-old Poppy, to a rented house in Sunninghill near Ascot, where a new life began. It was the end of one chapter and the beginning of a new one.

Lessons
1. Never be afraid to change course if it doesn't feel right.
2. If a family isn't working, you will find another, be it friends, colleagues or some other group.
3. Expect the unexpected.

CHAPTER 5

BEING MY OWN BOSS AND THE SACRIFICES OF WORKING LIFE

Understanding the Consequences of Success

A s a single mum in my early forties, I had left my marital home, with all its contents, and set up home in Sunninghill. I had made some of the most difficult decisions of my life but listened to my instinct. This is what freedom is all about.

Poppy and I loved our little home in the quaint village of Sunninghill. We felt so at home that I also moved my mum and dad from Wales to a bungalow two minutes' drive away. Our cosy palace was lovely but tiny, so poor Pops was moved into the box room to make space for the arrival of Kate the au pair. Kate was a Kiwi like me, so we hit it off immediately.

It couldn't have been easy living with us (or working for us for that matter!) but we seemed to get along and we made the best of our home on the hill. We had an open-plan kitchen, and we would spend all our time there—working, dancing and singing with no man telling any of us what to do. In fact, I think even the postman dared not come near! Before too long we adopted our first pet, Callie the cat with two legs and a walking stick. Poppy chose her. I wanted two kittens, Kate wanted Alfie, a fat old cat, but Poppy decided and Callie has been in her forever home ever since.

Laughter and Happy Days

If walls had ears, this house would have tales. But with all the drama, there was always laughter. These were our happy days. As a single mum and business owner, I would have liked a wife but opted for Kate the au pair instead. But however much help I received, it was never enough to take away the stress of all that responsibility of being a single mum with a business to run. When you own your own business, it's like having another baby. The demands never stop. Building a successful business has been one of my greatest accomplishments. It has also created some of my greatest challenges.

- I've worked in corporate, nursing and entrepreneurial roles, but owning your own business requires a completely different level of nerve and drive to survive and tell the tale.

Peter, my birth father, did his utmost to persuade me to remain in my corporate job, with all the trimmings and handcuffs that went with it. But being a business owner was in my genes—I got it from him after all!—and having the nerve to deal with it came with the prize.

Scary Moments

But this level of nerve is not for the faint-hearted and, with the uncertainty and pressure, it's hardly surprising that many businesses fail. According to the US Bureau of Labor Statistics (BLS) approximately 20 per cent of new businesses fail during the first two years; 45 per cent during the first five years; and 65 per cent during the first ten years. Only 25 per cent of new businesses make it to 15 years or more, and I can see why.

I have had far too many scary moments to mention, but my most frightening was when I didn't have the money to pay my team's wages. I had zero in the bank, and I didn't have a solution in mind. There was only one thing for it: I dropped down on to my knees and prayed.

To keep a business going year on year, with enough profit to keep Poppy and me fed and a roof over our heads, has not been easy.

My roles have included being the boss (with all the accountability); being the product while simultaneously delivering the service; being the subject-matter expert who designs the content; being the leader of the business and the team; and, last but not least, being the humble servant to the client. Behind the scenes, I know I must hit the numbers and keep in profit. For over ten years, I did this on my own and as a single parent—one of the hardest things I've ever done.

You might be thinking: why on earth did she put herself through that level of pressure while bringing up a little girl? Well, as with many of us working single mums, I had a mortgage and bills to pay, although I also desperately wanted to be there for my daughter. Happily, having my own business gave me the flexibility to take Poppy to school, put her to bed and mop her brow when she was unwell. Having spent my earlier career in corporate roles, on a plane or arriving at the office early and not leaving until late, when my daughter was born, I swore I'd have more choice.

Regardless of my decision to branch out on my own, the sacrifices I have made are no different from that of most working parents. At the end of the day, many of us do what we do in the workplace to make a better life for ourselves and the people we love.

- As a mother, I would do anything to give Poppy Hope a good life.

Jump off the Bus
Before you Combust

Apart from the basic requirement to pay the bills, having a passion for my work and delivering a great service keeps me going and feeling alive. When I get an idea in my head, and a vision of what is possible, I jump on the bus without any hesitation and drive, becoming excited about the journey with the mission fuelling the tank.

But with this passion comes risks: the danger of obsession, perfection and not letting go, keeping going for too long and of sacrificing your own needs for long working hours and keeping up the pace to beat the competition.

A bus of drive, ambition and mission-led focus is great. But, when overplayed, strength becomes weakness and, to prevent further deterioration, the bus needs to slow down—or you must jump off. This is one of the biggest issues someone faces in work, and the hardest thing for us to spot.

– Even when we love our job and love the ride, when the pressure is rising, we don't feel the heat until it's too late.

People said to me: "Why don't you get a job?", "What are you so stressed about?". Not many people understood or could even relate to the position I was in. Why would I give up something that I loved and worked so hard to build?

– It was hard and it almost broke me, but I was not ready to give up.

The Issue with Resilience and High Achievers

High achievers and resilient people are prone to stress because of the demands they put on themselves. But, for high achievers like me, it is less acceptable to admit this. Many of the leaders I work with are brave and strong people who are under the enormous pressure of having to cope with relentless uncertainty and organisational chaos at work. High achievers are human beings and not machines.

People who experience symptoms of stress and burnout are often the people who are the most committed. They just don't know when to stop. As a high achiever, I know the pain and struggles high performers face due to their strength. A willingness to take on responsibility, problem solving and having the ability to carry the burden of others are all wonderful leadership traits. Yet, these can have the biggest cost to the individual. Beneath the veneer of success, there are often powerful feelings that no-one wants to talk about.

With this in mind, it's hardly surprising that many successful people become stressed and worn out. When lows are reached, there is isolation, exhaustion and loss of joy and, with this, self-care goes out the window. At these times, showing any signs of vulnerability or asking for help is often seen as a complete no-no.

- Seeking help represents failure, and that is something that none of us ever want to face.

Stress and Burnout: the Biggest Risk Factors for Personal Failure

How(H)ever we cut it, stress is a silent epidemic and, if not faced and dealt with, it is also a silent killer. We all experience stress, uncertainty and difficulty in our working lives from time to time, and this is nothing to be ashamed of. However, there is still a massive stigma attached to it. Celebrities are constantly humiliated by the media for having mental health problems and not being able to cope with the pressure. Many of us are still shamed in the workplace and the community for these issues.

As a high-achieving people pleaser, I'd been in a survival state for too long, and like 80 per cent of the working population, I experienced symptoms of stress yet kept going. In my work as a corporate coach, I can honestly say that 80 per cent of the working population experience regular symptoms of stress. Fight, flight and freeze responses are present and apparent on a daily basis. These are the body's natural reaction to danger—inbuilt stress responses that help humans react to perceived threats, like a growling tiger or an avalanche. These are survival instincts which our ancestors developed many years ago, but they can cause unpleasant changes to our bodies and minds.

The symptoms of stress are shameful, too painful to admit, and behaviour rarely mentioned by those around us. Family members get the brunt of our frustrations and stress behaviour. Poppy used to say to me, "Mummy, your eyebrows are up," and that was a sure sign that I was stressed. I became more impatient, anxious, and even panic stricken at my worst. This wasn't me, the fun and adventurous Kiwi girl who didn't have a care in the world. I had become the stressed-out single mum who didn't have time to play any more. What an earth had happened in me in my forties? My quest for belonging and love had got out of hand, and my high-achieving people-pleasing traits had taken over. But I had to keep going because by then Poppy was at a private performing-arts school and there was no-one else to pay the fees.

Anyone worried about the impact of workplace stress on themselves or their family should listen to the signals, spot the red flags, and reach out for help before it's too late. I recommend that you read *When the Body Says No* by Gabor Maté (Wiley, 2011), one of my lifelong teachers, healers and a global expert on trauma and addiction. He explains that when our bodies are saying no, we continue to say yes. We don't listen; we don't notice; we just carry on, sometimes with the most horrendous consequences.

- Life is just too short.

Leadership is Lonely

When I look back, it wasn't the times when I didn't have any money that made me unhappy but the times when I was doing well. As my business grew, so did the problems and the pressure. By this time, Poppy and I had moved into a lovely house just down the road in Sunninghill. Poppy was having the time of her life at her performing-arts school, and living her dream of training to be an actor.

I had to be super focused on my work as well as meeting the needs of the budding performer, including driving her to Maidenhead before jumping on the train to London. Poppy was lucky and gifted enough to get several small roles in films and adverts—and I had to ferry her around the country inbetween client meetings and assignments.

Much of my work was in London, which meant getting on trains at ridiculous o'clock with no-one to share the child-rearing duties. The juggle was impossible, and the whole thing was quite absurd. As you can imagine, the needs of a pre-teen in drama school were never-ending. Most mothers I knew in my position had the support of a husband or a full-time nanny—and they were still all having meltdowns!

As I look back, this had to be the most stressful time of my life: my business was growing, my daughter was living the dream, but little old me was running the show all on my own. By then I had two wonderful PAs, Brittany and Amy, who helped look after the administration side of the business and the fallout of the juggle, including the three-legged cat.

– But at the end of the day, I was the boss, and they needed looking after too.

Leadership is lonely, and the journey surrounding it is full of dark holes, whether you are a leader of your own business, a CEO or a mum managing a home. All I wanted was a bit of company and someone to make me a cuppa.

Like most leaders in life, I had a list as long as my arm of endless problems to solve and tasks to complete.

I had no time for friendship or even a lunch date because I was working too hard to keep things afloat. I was living alone and surviving alone, and this was the most painful period of my life. I'd been in survival mode and on watch 24/7, sleeping underneath the window, keeping us safe, never really sleeping fully, just in case.

The business was becoming a tremendous success. But with my success came massive consequences, and for the first time in my life, I was feeling broken. Had I taken on more than I could chew?

Lessons
1. Being a business owner is like having a baby: the demands never stop.
2. Watch for signs of burnout, and slow down if necessary.
3. Leadership is lonely. Seek support.

CHAPTER 6

BREAKING THE CYCLE: A DOG, A MAN AND A CAMPER VAN

How to Change Things for the Better

When life takes a turn for the better, there is always a moment you will remember. In my case, I've had more than a few that I will never forget.

It takes a lot to break a cycle. We all get stuck in unhelpful cycles of behaviour, thought patterns, situations and even relationships that make us unhappy. We don't like what we're doing, we want to get out, but we feel trapped and we can see no way out. Cycles are a natural part of life, but when we get stuck in a pattern, it is tricky to break out and make an escape.

We all have things that we would like to change in our life—lose weight, make a career break, dye our hair, end a relationship. The list is endless. Sometimes it feels like we have no way out, and we just can't get past the point to create a new and happier life. But there is always hope, and whether it's a massive wake-up call or a gradual improvement, change is a process. It also requires a little luck.

So, there I was sobbing my heart out in a local café, sad, lonely and feeling sorry for myself when, as if by magic, in walked Emma, my new friend and life saver. I don't know about you, but I'm not in a habit of crying in public. This day was different. I was so sad and feeling so sorry for myself that I couldn't hold it in any more. I had reached the point of no return, and the tears were streaming down my blotchy face. I was a little girl lost who wanted to be loved and was fed up of being on my own.

A few waitresses walked by and looked down, trying not to catch my eye, not knowing what to do.

Then in came Emma, six feet something and unperturbed by my tears. She came right up to me, bent down and said, "It can't be that bad. I felt like that this morning. You can tell me if you like."

I couldn't believe it. Someone had seen me, a complete stranger, and been so kind. This is what I usually do for other people. I felt better immediately, my tears dried up and my heart lifted. This was already a wonderful friendship.

- As I reached the point on no return, my life started to turn.

Enter Fifi the Puppy

As a single mum and business owner with no-one to make my tea let alone help walk a dog, the idea of owning a puppy seemed impossible. After a while this dream became an obsession, though, so I started to take it seriously. Poppy had dreamed of going to drama school, and we made that happen. Why not this? I was torn between a little cute fluffy Maltese and a long-haired Pomeranian princess, but I couldn't make the final decision. Who on earth would look after this furry baby? Certainly not me with my London clients and being Poppy's taxi driver.

I had been looking for and dreaming of this dog for at least a year, if not two. In the cold and lonely nights, I would scroll through the Internet searching for a little white puppy but never quite mustering up the courage to go for it. In the end, it was Emma, my kind and loyal friend, who did it. "Just get the dog," was her advice. "I'll help you look after it." And that was that.

The very next day I took Poppy and her friend to look at the litter of little fluffy Maltese puppies. I wanted Bobo, the dopey-eyed cuddly one, Poppy's friend wanted Daisy, the bright sparky one. But in the end, we choose little Fifi. The thing about Fifi is that she is a free spirit, and that's exactly why Poppy picked her. Just like the rest of us in my family, mischievousness and autonomy rule, with a little separation anxiety thrown in. I had found the perfect dog, and little Fifi has been my freedom mascot ever since.

I had a knot in my stomach and didn't breathe for weeks. How would I cope with this mischievous little Fifi? She didn't sleep at night, and I was doing night shifts again, but as with all my crazy decisions, as soon as I'd committed, the how quickly revealed itself.

Fifi the dog made me realise that I was a good enough person and deserving of happiness.

And, with this realisation, and the decision to bring little Fifi home, my life changed forever.

The Tinder Bus

Not to dampen the romance or anything, but it has to be said that the dog came first and the boyfriend second. I hate to admit it, but at the same time as I was scrolling for a puppy, I'd occasionally have a look at Tinder. If you've ever been on that app, you'll know that it is quite different from looking for a puppy! As soon as I went on, I quickly jumped off. The men on there looking for fun were not cute or fluffy. Even so, I had the dream of a loving partner because beneath the veneer of the high-achieving, people-pleasing woman was a little girl on a quest for belonging and love. But such quests are never easy, and you must kiss a lot of frogs (or, in my case, Daves) before you find your prince.

It has to be said that it was Poppy who helped me find a man. She knew I secretly wanted a boyfriend, even though on the surface I was quite ambivalent about the whole affair. And now I had a dog, I was even less bothered. A couple of weeks after Fifi arrived, we had a weekend with the Pidgely family, staying with my wonderful friends Sarah, Andy, and Amelia. There Poppy was on it straightaway. She was set on finding her mum a boyfriend.

With her usual will and charm, she persuaded me to get back on the Tinder bus, swiping right in the hope of finding Mr Right. We all had a laugh, and within minutes I was chatting to a few Tinder hopefuls. Of course, before too long they showed their true colours. But this time, I didn't jump off straightaway. There was something keeping me on this bus.

Hope.

In Walks Dave the Ninth

A week went by, and just as I was about to throw in the towel, I swiped right with a tall, bald and rather kind-looking guy called David. He wasn't the usual type of man I'd go for, but with my history of men that was probably a good thing. I don't know what it was, but there was something I liked very much about his profile.

For a start, he was able to write and seemed to converse like a normal person. Not like some false fantasy character, throwing out a one-liner to try to hook me in.

Within a day, David got straight to the point and said that he would be available for a date. Would I like to meet him at the weekend? We exchanged numbers, and on 31 October 2018 we spoke for the first time. I was sitting in a restaurant in Paddington, a two-minute walk from where I was born, and I had a feeling I might have met my match.

So, with that, the ninth boyfriend called Dave walked in my life. Yes, I had previously had eight boyfriends called Dave. Although he says he doesn't count because he's not a 'Dave', he's David. (I think it does.)

When David arrived, and I opened the door, I knew he was lovely. I stumbled down the step, accidentally threw Fifi's water bowl all over him, handed him the dog and said, "Do you mind if she comes on our date?"

Without hesitation, he took the dog, held on to my hand and said, "Gosh, you look stunning. I'd love little Fifi to come on our date."

Good Things Come to Those who Wait

From that moment on, David has loved me like I've never been loved before. We have an equal relationship and meet each other's needs. David is organised and straight thinking, while I stick to what I know best and love him in any crazy way that I can. After my marriage broke up, it took ten years for me to want to live with a man again. Almost three years on, I can honestly say that I'm as happy as I can ever remember being.

When I look back to that day in October 2018, I was a bit all over the place. I definitely needed some love and care, and David was the man to do it. I know that sounds strange from an independent women like me, but let me explain: David literally loved me back to health again. Just like my mum. Through his love, patience and selfless care, I became me again. I really did need him, but in a healthy way because I knew he was good for me. My beautiful friend Ann Finlay spent the last few years praying for a big strong Scottish man to look after me and always being very specific in her prayers. He eventually came.

In the early days he had his hands full. By night, he would be chasing little Fifi around the garden trying to train her, at 6am he would literally throw me on the train with a cup of tea and then he'd have dinner waiting when I got home. All through the pandemic, he would cook the meals, do the shopping and carry out all the nurturing duties.

Many of my friends would say "David cooking again? You are so spoilt Jenny!" and all their husbands would frown and mutter "You're letting the side down here, Dave". But he didn't care. It would just encourage him to do more.

The News I Never Expected—I had ADHD

I had been so worn out and exhausted by coping on my own that this man was not only making me happy but he was helping me get my life back in order. I suppose I had got into a bit of a pickle with my living arrangements, but Poppy and I thought it was normal to live in a bit of chaos, and so long as we were happy and having fun, we really didn't care.

I've always enjoyed having fun, and I've always been a little impulsive. I just thought it was all part of my creative nature, and I suppose it is. But when I was at school, I also struggled to concentrate and focus on anything I found boring.

In my fifties, I decided that maybe there was a reason for all these traits after attending a lecture about ADHD for work. As I was sitting in the lecture, the psychiatrist started talking about the traits of someone with this condition. I kept putting my hand up like a schoolgirl in a classroom. "Yes, that's just like me!" I said. I couldn't believe what I was hearing. Everything fitted. Before long, I couldn't bear it any more. "Oh, my goodness. I think I've got ADHD!" I blurted out.

And with this shocking thought, I immediately phoned my good friend Eugene, who knows all about ADHD from his work in the pharma industry. In his warm and kind manner, he gently recommended that I might like to get an assessment. I knew nothing about ADHD other than the basics, and never in a million years had I suspected I might have it. In my usual style, I did my research and hunted down the best specialist psychiatrist I could find: Dr Cubbin, who's specialty is women with ADHD.

The ADHD assessment is quite a long process, with thorough investigations involving medical and school records. David even had to speak to Dr Cubbin and 'give evidence' on what it was like living with me. Fortunately for me, the report from David to Dr Cubbin was glowing, other than that I found it difficult to complete some tasks, got distracted easily and had been promising to make him a cup of coffee for the last three months. It had never arrived. They laughed and agreed it was probably better for him to keep making his own for the time being.

I was formally diagnosed in August 2020, and I can honestly say that it has been one of the best things that has ever happened to me, even though ADHD is at the bottom of the neurodiversity pile and is probably the most misunderstood of conditions on the spectrum—and the one with the worst reputation. I am proud to have the diagnosis of ADHD. It helps me to make sense of me and explains why I do certain things. For years I've been criticised and belittled for being like a magpie (attracted to new and shiny things) or for having a "scattered mind" (a very rude description coined by the most horrible boss of my life).

But I'd rather have these traits and a diagnosis of ADHD than not because I know that as long as I get some order, the world is my oyster and I have a good chance of achieving whatever I put my mind to.

The Fall Before
the Freedom Bus

Fast forward from August 2020 to August 2021. Aged 52. During this period something happened that was so horrendous in my life that it broke me beyond my normal coping point. I will not talk about it now and will never talk about it again. All you need to know is that I had my final lesson before my freedom bus arrived.

When I started this chapter, I said that it takes a lot to break a cycle. It might be a wake-up call, it might be a small change and, in all cases, it's always a process. What happened to me in this period of my life was such a shock that it catapulted me into change. I had no choice. Along with all the love and good things that had come my way, this was one of the worst things that have ever happened to me.

As I was clawing my way back to sanity, I fortunately had David by my side, who in true David style loved me back to me again. I had lost a stone in weight, stopped working and was gently easing myself back into life again, but this time everything seemed different. Little did I know that nothing would be the same again. This breakdown was the breakthrough that I needed. I had reached a point where I had nothing to lose, so I decided to put myself at the front of the queue.

By then I had Fifi and I had David. Then finally, in June 2021, a long wished for camper van arrived. With all dreams, we hope they'll bring us freedom. In my case, all three did.

Lessons

1. Listen to your wishes and make them happen.
2. You deserve happiness.
3. You can break the cycle.

PART 2

ALL ABOARD
THE FREEDOM BUS

CHAPTER 7

MAKING PEACE
WITH MY PAST

Lessons from Adoption and my Quest
for Belonging and Love

My career choices are all related to the essence of who I am: a mischievous and adventurous girl who wants to love and be loved and relishes having fun.

Throughout life, I have also been gifted with the ability to sprinkle all the difficulties I have faced with a sparkly light of hope. My life experiences so far have made me who I am, and it is through the pain and sometimes downright misery that what I consider to be miracles have occurred.

As a warrior in my life, the struggles, trauma and hurt might have broken me temporarily. But I have always got back up again and been grateful for the lessons learnt and gifts received.

It's not the successes that have given me the best bits; the greatest pain and difficulties have made me who I am.

It is the gifts from the suffering that have helped me transform and grow, rather than what's been handed to me on a plate. Through my pain and healing, I have been able to help others with theirs. It just works like that. We can only help people with things that we've been through or if we have gained enough experience and skill to accompany others on their journey.

Facing the Truth—When I Stopped Lying to Myself

I never realised I had half the problems I had until they were staring me in the face or knocking at my door so loudly that I couldn't ignore them any more.

Stress is a perfect example of this. When we're stressed, we don't feel good, and we then behave in ways that make others feel miserable. You could be in a relationship with an unsafe person, in a job that makes you unhappy, or have addictions that are slowly killing you. All of these things cause us to act negatively towards others. But regardless of the level of stress behaviour, or the tolerance of those around us, we still carry on thinking that it's everyone else's problem.

So how should we address this? Well, wake up, smell the roses and stop lying to yourself.

This is much easier said than done, of course, and it took me over 50 years to have this realisation, with a lot of mistakes and repeated falls along the way—more than would fit into this book. It took me to the ripe old age of 51 to fully admit my weakness, a lifetime to stop overachieving and over-pleasing all the time.

So please don't feel that I'm being harsh when I say this. I'm just saying it how it is. We must be clear about the problems we are faced with and have the courage to look them in the eye. This is the hardest bit and the step that many of us miss—but if you want the key to be free, these are the steps you must take.

– If we lie to ourselves, we cannot be ourselves.

It always puzzles me why it's easier to see other people's mistakes than spot our own. But when we are in a negative mindset or situation, we sometimes cannot see it and we are often part of the problem. It's difficult to get an outsider's perspective. Therefore, it's useful to have safe and loving people around us so that we can relax and be ourselves.

Our egos can't bear to admit that we are weak, wrong or imperfect and will do anything to protect our reputations, blaming others instead. Many of us find it difficult to admit when we reach a sticking point. That's if we notice at all, of course. Often problems must become so big that they hit us over the head and say "If you don't deal with this, your life might be over" before we wake up and take notice.

Regardless of race, gender or creed, we all have stuff to deal with. As far as I'm concerned, no-one is immune. When I share this with my clients, I call this simple fact 'normalising'. It reminds us all that we're not going crazy, and if we are, then many others have also lost the plot! When we understand ourselves and acknowledge we have something that needs attention, we are halfway to solving the problem. I call this the process of 'getting things off the table'.

Facing the Truth is the Key to a Successful Life

Imagine you have a table in front of you. It might have a white tablecloth, see-through glass or be made of solid wood. The task is to take a good look at your life and place all your current problems out in front of you. Be honest. What are the difficulties? List them one by one.

The next step is to prioritise the top three, name them and do the work to take them off the table so we can get on with our lives. A clean table is like an uncluttered mind—all the white noise is replaced with clear space for possibility and transformation to emerge.

Facing our deepest issues and being vulnerable enough to feel pain and grief is probably one of the most difficult things you will do.

But whether the issues are from the past, present or future, facing them is the key to a free and meaningful life.

– Freedom + meaning = success

Avoiding the pain because we just can't go there ensures that it remains, and we get stuck. But you are not alone. We all need a hand to hold when facing our greatest pain and problems. That's where community, love and belonging come in.

From I to We
—More Together Than Alone

— When we realise we are all connected we don't
feel so ashamed and alone.

This is the wonderful thing about community, friendship and any form of support network. It is a place where we can go with other people like us and say, "Oh my goodness, did that happen to you? I thought I was the only one." I am a big fan of therapy, coaching and any safely run process that accompanies us to heal our pain and help us make peace with our history. Helping make sense of our world and be witnessed in our pain is one of the most beneficial things anyone can do. Whether that be in a one-to-one friendship or therapy session, or a safe support group. It is in this space that we see reflections of ourselves, and we can make sense of our issues together.

— When we feel safe and held by another, we are
able not only to heal together but we can also
co-create our future.

So, before we go further down the road to freedom, let me share some of the issues that I've got off the table.

1. From Rejection to Letting go of Expectation
One of the greatest lessons to come out of all of my experiences arises from *Rejection*, which—at birth, or any

time in life—hurts. We all need to feel wanted, included and heard. But sometimes people want you and sometimes they don't—and that may have nothing to do with you. After all, they have their lives, too.

Within a family, we all have a place and with that comes a natural feeling of entitlement: we believe it is our right to belong in that system regardless of what others think. Being rejected from your family system brings pain, but that does not give you the right to think that people want you in that place, nor that your family should want you no matter what.

I am ashamed to admit it, but I've spent many years not enjoying 6 March. My birthday. I secretly wanted to hear from Lorraine, saying that she wanted a relationship with me after all. There I was on my special day, waiting for her simple message: *Happy birthday, Jenny.* I got lucky for a few years. It might have only been a one-liner on Facebook, but it was enough to satisfy the little baby inside, waiting patiently for her mother.

Eventually I learnt that this wanting and waiting just perpetuated the pain. It's like any relationship that you have where you are anticipating more—a bit more romance, a little more love; a sign that we are good enough, worthy enough. I was living a lie, but I couldn't let go of the hope.

I stopped waiting on a day I'll never forget. It was 5:30am on my forty-eighth birthday, and I woke up and searched for the Facebook message. It wasn't there. And, from that moment, I knew that it wasn't coming and would never do so again. Something happened then: my grief was released and the pain came, first in a wave and then in a storm that didn't stop. Nobody could console me. I cried and cried, and it was as if every cell in my body was ready to set its pain free. This was a turning point for me, and I never wanted to feel like it again.

Too much expectation leads to great disappointment. You must lower your expectations or have none, otherwise you will be condemned to have an endless appointment with disappointment. Waiting for someone else to deliver has been one of my biggest mistakes. I finally realised that I must not keep wanting and waiting for that which is not there, scrabbling around for a few crumbs from the table. You are better off baking the cake.

Giving birth to me was a huge decision for Lorraine in her circumstances. I could not, and should not, have expected more. It's easy to take our birthright for granted, and so much easier to blame someone else when it goes wrong.

In the end, the greatest rejection can come from yourself. But if there's one thing that adoption has taught me, it's that I don't need to wait for anyone's approval to exist. I was given a life, and that is the biggest gift I could ever have received.

2. From People Pleasing to Loving Myself

It's certainly human nature to want to be loved and to fit in. But when this is the driving force, it can get you into quite a few difficulties. It's often said that the hardest task for us all is simply to love ourselves—and it is true.

The sentiments that surround feelings of rejection lead naturally to my second life lesson, that of *People Pleasing,* or rather how not to be a people pleaser. This is a journey during which you cleanse yourself of doubts/negative thoughts and 'energy vampires'—all the rubbish in life you have put up with because you don't feel that you deserve better. Instead, you start to accentuate the positives by being with people and in places that make you feel good about yourself.

It's a journey that begins with the issues of over-giving, over-needing and overachieving for approval. With this over-giving of yourself comes a lack of strength at your individual boundary: the physical and psychological line of self that separates us from each other; where 'I' begin and 'others' end. I've always felt I've had to stretch myself beyond myself because being me was never enough. If I work hard, be good and make everyone happy, I might be good enough to keep.

When I look back at my life, I realise that low self-esteem and low self-worth all stem from one thing: you don't feel that you matter, and so the flow of love to yourself is blocked. When you are unable to love yourself, it is the most natural thing to look outside to find love from others.

In fact, there are many ways in which I've done this, but it's largely been an external over-giving fix such as achieving at work, being a winner and even hanging around with people who were not really that good for me.

Sometimes people take advantage of this vulnerability and need for external love. They can spot it a mile away. These people come in many guises, and I have met more than enough to know that I have been an easy target. They think they can get away with murder, treating me any way they like because they sense that I don't think much of myself. Indeed, my dad said to me recently: "Jenny, your kind nature has got the better of you, and people have always taken advantage."

Nowadays, if my natural kindness does create problems, I will say to others: "No, it is not okay to treat me in that way." Through understanding the negative effects of over-giving, I have gained the ability to stop pleasing people—and started pleasing myself instead.

Recently I found a dusty old photo of me that had been tucked away in a drawer for years. A little girl in a bonnet looking sweet and shy. Despite her lack of confidence, you can still spot a determined look in her eye. This is a girl seeking adventure. It reminded me of who I've always been. She was always there underneath all the self-doubt and desire for acceptance. She just forgot how to be who she was. I cherish that little girl and am thankful for the journey that has taken me from the girl who thought that she didn't matter to the most magical girl in the world (in my eyes!). She is the only person I need to please now.

3. From Trauma and Shame to Healing the Pain

The human condition ensures that we all experience *Trauma* at some time in our lives. We are all survivors on one level or another, but the most painful of all is the hidden trauma which triggers *Shame*. And the greatest calamity is that, through our pain, we disconnect from ourselves and don't know we've done it. We just can't face the agony.

In my case, I've been riddled with shame but didn't even realise it. I was used to hiding and splitting myself into parts so that I was accepted and connected with others at the expense of being connected with myself. This is the conflict between the need to belong and being yourself.

Trauma shapes your brain, and we see an image of the world through this lens. Until we process it and come back into loving connection with ourselves, the dysfunctional dynamics and attachment patterns will play out in our lives until we're healed. Even though there is nothing wrong with us, trauma can give us a shame-based view of ourselves and the world which makes us feel we've done something wrong. Shame makes us feel so horrible that we hide away until it pops up, completely by surprise.

Sadly, this disconnection from ourselves and our pain can cause us to connect with others in unhealthy and dysfunctional ways, living out the very patterns which we've spent so long trying to hide from. There are many techniques we use to avoid feeling our pain, including trying to numb it, distraction and avoidance. If you find you are running away from yourself, take it from me, this is quite normal and a natural survival response. Trauma is a wound, and its scar tissue is hard. Although protective, it is rigid, inflexible and doesn't grow. When we feel safe and loved enough to face our trauma, and heal through our pain, we soften, stop hiding away and become whole and alive again.

4. From Ambivalence and Anxiety to Authentic Attachment

Fear that you will lose a relationship can be ever-present, particularly if you have an anxious attachment style and the thought of abandonment drives you insane. This was my experience for many years. Many of us trade in our true selves for the sake of attachment, but the saddest thing is that, in doing so, we often continue to put up with horrible things that stunt our growth and keep us from moving on.

There is a dynamic which occurs between being our true authentic selves in relationships and our desire to maintain these relationships—and this is what I call the *Authentic Relationship Dilemma*. We need attachment—to be loved and held, to feel safe and secure—while also needing to be true to ourselves. This plays out in the normal teenage experience of pulling away from the attachment of our parents and discovering who we are. This is difficult for teenagers because parents often can't let go or handle teenage separation, rebellion and anger. But it is the parents who often face the greatest problem because they've forgotten how to be themselves.

Many babies develop attachment issues from their relationships with their mothers, through no fault of the mother or the child. This often happens without anyone realising it. Maybe the mother is distracted, avoidant or anxious, but for whatever reason, this rubs off on how the infant copes with life.

Perhaps because of my early experience, I developed a pattern of both *Anxious Attachment* (not wanting to be abandoned) and *Ambivalent Attachment*, where I said: "Don't worry, I can do it by myself." I know now that none of this is healthy, but it was not my fault. Since I've developed a healthy attachment with myself and healed my hurts, I only cultivate healthy relationships in which I can thrive and be myself.

> **Lessons**
> 1. Face the truth: we can't change problems unless we see them.
> 2. Use a good support network to help you, be it family, friends, therapists, or others.
> 3. Identify the lessons specific to your life. Use them to help you to grow.

CHAPTER 8

THE DRAMA AND DYNAMICS OF THE WORKPLACE FAMILY

Lessons from Corporate Life

As the founder of Feel Good Leadership, the company I started in 2009, and within my role as a corporate leadership coach, I've spent over 30 years helping people solve their personal and professional issues. And this has given me a huge insight into what makes us tick. My skills, knowledge and experience are equally relevant to any human being because the issues of leadership are the issues of life.

– From the boardroom to the psychiatric ward, human issues are much the same.

My work has taken many turns over the years, but my passion remains the same: relating to people as human beings, listening to their stories and assisting in their hour of need. Nothing makes me happier than helping people feel good and achieve their dreams. Generally, people that I work with hire me because they like me, they trust me and I give them what they need.

My career has not been dissimilar to many in the corporate world. The difference perhaps is that, as well as enthusiasm for the task at hand, I've had a parallel passion for people, doing what's right and speaking the truth. This has put me in some tricky spots with tough consequences but none that I haven't been able to handle without too much bother.

During my 30 years in business and corporate life, I've come to a profound understanding of the real issues people face in the workplace, and it's on this depth of insight that I base a large part of my work. Knowing how to resolve conflict, and understanding how family and organisational systems work, all helps.

Where there are people, there is drama, and it is the relationship dynamics, and dysfunctions, of work and family life that get us all in the end.

– Workplace issues are human issues, and not one of us is immune.

Problems at work can be complex and extremely difficult to handle, even for the best of us. Luckily, most of the issues we experience at work are resolvable—even if that means finding another job.

In many respects, there is no better way to think about the issues facing organisations than in terms of families. The problems families face domestically are mirrored in offices, factories and other work hubs. And, as with any system, they are full of history, complexity, challenge and change.

An excellent example could be seen in the very public breakdown in relations between the Duke and Duchess of Sussex and the royal family which emerged in 2020. The problems underlying Harry and Meghan's spectacular rift with the British monarchy caused an international sensation. But their problems are ones all families face, including our work families in commerce and industry.

We all have a bit of drama in our lives, whether we like it or not. If you have a role in any social system, be that work or family, the chances are that you will encounter some difficulties. Below are just some of the problems that can occur.

Imbalances of Power

I t is the most natural thing in the world to want to be yourself and have a place in the group. This doesn't mean that you must be the boss, but at least have a place where you can settle. When the power is unfair, we are not acknowledged, and people have power over us. We are made to feel small, worthless and undervalued, and these nuances in power are extremely destructive. This happens at all levels of organisational life, regardless of seniority.

The Unspoken Roles
and Belonging Rules

There are many unspoken things that we are expected to do in a social system. It's a bit like inviting certain friends to a party. One gets the party started; another does the washing up. These are the unspoken rules of belonging in the group.

We often talk of them, and do know they are there, and we are pulled to do them as they are what keeps us included in the group. Whether we like it or not, we are compelled.

Sometimes we find ourselves doing things that we wouldn't normally do because that's what is expected. We don't want to do these things, but we are stuck within the system and feel we have no choice: working at weekends, meetings running over, gossiping, playing golf.

Exclusion

This is one of the most painful things that can happen to us. It is rejection from a group that we belong to. It comes in many forms, and often it's not obvious when it's happening. Therefore, we feel bad, although it's difficult to put our finger on why.

Not including, pushing out, ignoring, sidelining, blanking, not listening to, talking over, minimising—the message is this: you don't belong here; you are not welcome as you; you are not valued enough in your role to have a say or even to stay here at all.

Hierarchy

We all work in systems of hierarchy, and we all have a place. We might not like that place in the hierarchy, and we might do anything to get on top. We might jump into someone else's place and act as if it is ours. Different places have different weightings and values in all systems, depending on the purpose of the group and weighting put on the value of the role. In a family system in the Western world, there is a higher weighting on the person who earns the money and their agency rather than the one who has a nurturing, caring role. Nurses get paid a low wage; investment bankers earn a high wage. The place in the hierarchy is dependent on where the system puts the power.

Ultimately, we are social animals and trying our best to survive. However good and functional our organisation is, the game is tough and full of people trying to make sense of their place and do their jobs to the best of their ability.

Office Politics
and Playground Tactics

As mentioned, my interest in what makes people tick started at an early age with my job at the nursing home and later at an insurance firm. The insurance firm brought my first experience of office politics, as I was left out of the in-group thanks to one woman in particular. This left me feeling miserable. So, in my normal style, I summoned the courage and asked straight out: "Have I done something to upset you, Angela?"

She stuttered, and I detected a kinder look in her eye. Then she admitted, "I'm sorry. I didn't realise that it made you feel like that." We became as friendly as we could after that, and I no longer came to work dreading what Angela might be saying behind my back.

Now, while organisational life isn't always as simple as that, this first encounter taught me a lot about the workplace—that the dynamics are not dissimilar to those of the playground and can be just as hurtful. I quickly learnt to say it how it is. I don't let sleeping dogs lie, and when I see people being mean, I step in to seek resolution. I've never been afraid to walk into a storm and face up to what's going on. Hurt feelings are hard to see, and we rarely know how we've hurt other people unless they tell us.

At this point, let me make it clear that I am no innocent. Alongside my optimism and peace-making ways, there is an equal dose of ego and competitiveness, along with a passion for achieving great things. I've caused arguments, not backed down, been called defiant and I'm embarrassed to say that I have not always handled myself with dignity and grace, particularly when hurt and wounded.

So, none of us is perfect, and in organisations, whether as the boss of yourself or others, the business life is hard, with achieving and making gains at the core of many of our roles. It's hardly surprising that we all learn ways to achieve this by defeating others, which sometimes involves playing a dirty game to survive and to avoid getting burnt. But as I've always said to my daughter: the playground bully is usually hurting themselves the most.

– Do not tolerate being treated badly and set your own boundaries of what is acceptable and what is not.

Toxic Work Cultures and Bad Behaviour

Whether behind closed doors or in an open boardroom, I've witnessed people at their worst. Be it in an acute psychiatric wing or a corporate setting, the behaviour is the same. We are all vulnerable and, even while being treated horribly by others, none of us is immune to behaving badly. The biggest issue is when low-level or harmful behaviour is accepted and tolerated as it then becomes the norm.

I know better than anyone the issues that people face in organisations and in leadership teams. They all boil down to behaviour: behaviour that brings out the best in us and that which doesn't.

As we are all waking up to the impact of toxic cultures and questionable behaviour that is no longer acceptable—the Me Too movement is one example—the light is being shone on things that we once thought were okay or we didn't have a full awareness of. With this awakening, we find the information needed to take action to bring about change.

It is not only the 'survival of the fittest' instinct that makes us behave in horrible ways. Stress affects our brains. It changes us, makes us ill and turns us into people we no longer recognise. I have seen this in myself and others. But it is how we say sorry and heal that is the key.

Feel Good Leadership was born when I decided to give my business a new focus and life. The name came to me after I had been badly hurt by a personal business coach I had been seeing. He thought it was good to put so much pressure on someone that they broke down and were reduced to tears. Anyone with an ounce of understanding would know that this is totally unskilled and, in fact, absurd. I wanted my business to be the opposite, to make people feel good.

Sadly, in the business world, this coach's type of approach is not unusual, and in life generally there are many preying on the vulnerable and taking advantage. This isn't making a mistake; it is cold-blooded and nasty. In such cases, the questions to ourselves must be: 'Is this behaviour driven by power and personal gain or equality, respect and integrity?' and 'Why on earth didn't I spot it before?'

I drove off from the last meeting I had with this coach, on a baking hot day in August, with tears streaming down my face and my car's air conditioning not working. I was so upset that I made two of the biggest decisions of my life: to rename my business and buy a new car. The former proved a good decision; the latter was not.

- Notice how others' behaviour makes you feel.
  How do you behave when you are stressed?
  Are you rude or short tempered? Do you have low emotional self-regulation?

The Boss is Always Right, and the Privilege of Power

Why would someone with the privilege of power (and my money) use it so badly and cause so much upset?

This behaviour is quite difficult to spot as it's often subtle, and even accepted and encouraged in some quarters. But how on earth could anyone perform at their best when someone they trust places a knife to their back? It's really an issue involving human rights, neglect and betrayal, and sadly I have seen it and experienced it more times than I care to mention.

The trouble is that when you are treated like this in the workplace, the idea of 'the boss is always right' comes into play. The boss will almost always win in any situation. This is so subtle that I often have to help people to understand it, and it is something that many find difficult to accept.

Parentification—I'm in Charge Here. I Know Best

Thinking that you know better than your boss or could do a better job is called 'parentification'. This is a useful systemic perspective from my training and is applicable to organisational systems as well as families.

There are many reasons for this, but typically it comes about when there is a gap in the space above, a historical loss or an unoccupied seat.

In family life, for example, if the grandmother love is missing, or the mother is being pushed out, or disrespected, or absent, the child steps into the mother's place and begins to think that they know best.

Exactly the same thing happens in organisational life. The boss is the boss and the mother is the mother. They might not have been occupying their place too well, or even have left it empty for a while. This means that there is always a possibility that others move into this space and push them out the way. And this is wrong. As children should not be telling their parents what to do, neither should we disrespect our boss.

Happily, in all my years of working life I've only had one experience of a horrible boss. (This boss also discriminated against my neurodiversity.) On the day he started, he took an instant dislike to me and immediately insulted me.

Being the person I am, I tried everything I could to get this man to like me and show him I was good at my job. I even tried to understand why he took this turn against me. But the bottom line was this: he didn't like me, he disrespected me until I left and there was absolutely nothing I could do about it other than leave.

The mistake I made was not to spot it sooner. But when you're in it, you can't see it. And that's the story of all of our lives at one point or another.

I'd enjoyed four wonderful years with the previous boss and had an excellent reputation in the organisation, but as soon as this new boss took over, my life was in ruins and life in this company was over.

I don't feel bad about it, though, because all good things come to an end. I took this experience (with lots of additional training in conflict resolution and mediation) and now help others in similarly disempowered positions to speak up and regain their power.

- Avoid people who make you feel bad and treat you with disrespect. And if this is accepted by the system, get out quick!

Losing Our Place and the Fall from Grace

The leaders I work with are hard core. They've trained for years on the organisational battleground and are much better at this game than I could ever be. Yet they get broken, squashed and hurt like anyone else. They just don't show it—not to the outside world at any rate. A leader might be at the top of their game but, like all of us, they can lose their crown in the end.

However smart, strong and brave, none of us in any position is immune to losing our place or falling from grace. I have seen the most extraordinary leaders stripped of their stripes overnight and, however unfair, this can happen at the most unexpected times. If it's never happened to you, please have compassion and understanding for those for whom it has.

From being in the in-group, the smartest can be banished to become the outsider, power ripped from beneath their feet. You can be the star of the show or the CEO but the position never lasts. There is always someone ready and willing to take your place, and soon your name becomes a distant memory. Stripped of your place, abused or shamed, it may take you a while to recover. But take it from me, with patience and time, you can rise again a whole lot wiser.

- No-one is invincible, and it could be your head on the chopping board next.
- If you have a fall, accept the gift of humility.
- Treat people well as you rise because they may be fundamental if you fall.

Ambiguity and Confusion

Ambiguity and confusion run through most organisational systems and these are among the most sticky and difficult issues we face. But we often feel ashamed of being confused, and a lack of clarity and control are among our greatest social fears. When confusion and ambiguity are long-lasting, we easily lose our footing and confidence in our ability. This is one of the biggest problems that can derail or hijack even the most successful-looking plan. A lack of clarity from any leader can have devastating effects, and that's why getting to the bottom of this is so critical for success.

Confusion turns up in many shapes and sizes and, although perhaps obvious to the outsider, within the system it can be harder to spot. It can take the form of unclear structures and operating models, or a lack of governance. It can also be postponing or adding to things, or even moving the goalposts. All this creates uncertainty and, in its extreme form, can lead to gaslighting or distorting someone's reality.

Creativity and authenticity all arise from confusion and ambiguity, and this is the place that possibility arises. The trouble is that we don't like existing in a place of uncertainty because it makes us feel anxious. We prefer structure and logic and linear thinking (well most of us anyway). In organisations, we don't like confusion because it makes us feel stupid, uncomfortable and it takes up too much time. It takes a strong leader to make the time to tolerate confusion without displaying a lot of frustration.

- Know that if you feel confused, there is a high chance everyone else does too. Become more comfortable with confusion. Seek clarity but do not push it too soon.
- Keep digging and don't give up. You are not stupid; you are only human. All the best things come out of mess.

Nuance and Cover-up

Confusion is riddled with nuance and cover-up, all adding to our loss of control, and this can lead in some cases to workplace bullying.

The trouble is that no-one wants to see or admit that a mess exists because we are ashamed about the confusion or not coming up with the answers.

Our ego and pride act as a protective shell which stops success and stifles the truth. In many systems that I work in, the true problems cannot be seen or faced because that would cause more problems than they're worth. So many issues, and their root causes, stay hidden until the leader and the system are ready to see them.

My job in these situations is to respond with warmth and understanding and offer the process of perspective and of challenging the norm and previously held assumptions. It takes a gentle, patient approach to help people uncover the nuance, and the shame, of not seeing what has been hidden. When we view things as they really are, we must overcome the disbelief and lack of awareness of not seeing these problems before. It takes careful unpicking and gentle discovery to see the systemic dynamics at play.

Throughout my career listening to people, it's become clear that confusion and mess coexist with clarity and success. And one of the biggest secrets is this: the smartest and most successful leaders are often confused and disorientated, with many suffering sleepless nights at one time or another.

- There are no shortcuts, and it is only from this mess and ambiguity that clarity, sense and the best ideas arise.
- Notice subtle cues and micro-aggressions.
- Focus on your leadership lens, widen your perspective and be the change you want to see.

The Fear of Speaking up

You can see how the issues mount up: not having your voice heard, bullying, blame and shame, attitudes of team members, exclusion, confusion, power struggles.

One really crucial issue, which can perhaps be the most damaging, is the fear of speaking up and a toxic culture of silence. Put simply, this is 'not saying it how it is'. There are three main reasons why people don't talk: ambiguity and uncertainty; power dynamics—'It's not my place to challenge the boss'; and social threat—people feel intimidated into not holding a counter view. The tendency to speak up, or not, also comes down to whether a person feels powerless, excluded or uncertain in a social system.

The SCARF model is a useful frame to look at how people act in a social system and why it's so difficult to speak out. This describes the five key domains of social threat and reward: Status, Certainty, Autonomy, Relatedness and Fairness. People will speak up in difficult situations only if they perceive a low threat level. Or, in the language of SCARF, they speak up if doing so won't overwhelmingly threaten their sense of status and relatedness.

For three months in 2014, Mona Weiss was in a hospital surrounded by anesthesiologists, nurses and surgeons. She was there not for treatment but for her own research. Weiss was studying an aspect of organisational psychology known as employee voice—the phenomenon of workers speaking up when they see or hear something that troubles them. In any given workplace, there are people with lesser voices (those who largely keep to themselves) and others with greater voices (those who usually make their thoughts known).

She found that the tendency to speak up or not comes down to whether a person feels powerless, excluded or uncertain in a social system. In addition, survey data indicates that the majority of employees, 75 per cent, have experienced workplace bullying or harassment, which can lead to a toxic, low-performing work environment. Only a small fraction ever speak up about it.

Opportunities to speak up are missed. We don't intervene before it's too late and we don't call out damaging behaviour. How many mistakes are not corrected? How many times have high emotions derailed conversations? How often is questionable behaviour not addressed? This latter aspect is even more apparent in the online world of video meetings, where it is even less easy to call someone out. We all know how hard it is to speak up when you know you're going to get shut down or not be heard. We freeze and can't get the words out. Then, when we do, they come out all wrong, bringing shame upon ourselves for not speaking up properly and not managing to have our say.

- Not speaking up, or leaders not listening, has huge consequences.

Why is allowing and supporting people to speak up so important? Because by voicing actual or potential problems you challenge the status quo, existing behaviour and open up the possibility of sharing new ideas. Speaking up allows for a course correction to the direction of travel. It increases collaboration, inclusion, innovation and leads to all-round better teamwork. To help people find their voice, we must reduce the fear of using it by:

- Speaking up in a way that is less challenging for the speaker, and less threatening to the person being spoken to.
- Making speaking up feel less threatening and maybe even rewarding. By doing this leaders can create the kind of culture in which psychological safety thrives.
- Validating and acknowledging what others say. Even if you disagree, you can still acknowledge.

The power of acknowledgment is profound. When we hear others and acknowledge what they say, it gives us all power and validation and provides a place for diversity. It is with that authenticity of voice and equality of power that we all win. As one.

Lessons

1. Workplace issues are human issues. Treat everyone with respect.
2. Do not tolerate being treated badly, and don't be afraid to name it or leave.
3. Speak up, and listen and acknowledge others.

CHAPTER 9

SHARING STRUGGLES AND THE ROAD TO POSSIBILITY

Coaching Techniques: an Unorthodox Approach

People started sharing their personal issues and secrets with me at 13 years old, if not before. I'm just one of those listening souls who makes time to understand. There I was with my head down a toilet, trying to earn £4 an hour, and Mr Trenaman, the poshest patient on the block, would not stop talking to me. "Jenny, my daughter's coming in later. What do you think I should say?", "Shall I wear the grey cravat or the blue one?", "My shoulder is so painful. Can you come and have a look?".

For goodness's sake, I would think, I'm only 13 and it's gone past my lunch break!

I was always late and often missed my lunch because I was too busy listening to the patients' problems and getting distracted by the stories of their lives. I would much rather sit and chat and listen to their woes than get on with a boring task. And this is the story of my life.

Since having my head down a toilet, I've occupied a number of professions which involved listening, understanding and helping people work through their personal issues. From toilet cleaner and time-share seller to psychiatric nurse and executive coach, all roads led to the same destination—listening to people's problems and helping them sort them out. If there was a *Mastermind* on how to solve a human problem, I'd stand a good chance of winning. Mind you, if I had any general knowledge subject, that would be a completely different matter!

The Secrets From 35 Years of Listening and Understanding

I hold the secrets of thousands of humans from over 35 years of listening and offering advice. Like all therapists, psychologists and counsellors, I have a brain vault where things go within a bank of universal understanding. I make patterns and connections with all this information. This enables me to understand human behaviour, most of which seems normal to me.

Having such an enormity of human data enables me to be as sharp as a button when it comes to solving both simple and complex issues. But of course before the rabbit, or the magic solution, comes out of the hat, we need to see the problem, face it, and process it—and that is the tricky bit which most of us avoid.

My working life has been dedicated to learning, loving and helping people.

I've failed, I've upset people and I've done things badly on more than one occasion. But I've never been afraid of saying sorry, always reflected and grown, and I've always dug deep to understand and better myself and be kinder to others.

I have trained to within an inch of my life to better understand human beings and what we can do to acknowledge and deal with our pain.

Along with all the training in nursing, psychiatry, neuroscience, conflict resolution and Systemic Constellations (more of which later), fundamentally I have learnt the hard way by practising first on myself.

A fancy title or status makes no difference to me. Whether I work with the CEO of a multinational company or a single mother at a food bank…

- … we are human first and leaders second, and we all have a choice about how we behave and treat our colleagues.

We cannot control how others lead their lives, so we must stay focused on how we lead ourselves and our own lives and always strive to be better.

- Not one of us is better than another.

Truth and Kindness Take
us to Another Level

Truth is an ongoing conversation about things that matter, conducted with passion, integrity, and discipline. If we want to live with the truth, we must live in the moment because the conversations keep changing and so does the truth.

I have always been persistent in seeking the truth. I am never afraid of jumping into a storm (or even causing it!). I am Truth Finder, Storm Chaser and Catalyst for Change all in one. I lead with my heart and use my head for assistance, being disruptive, constructive and kind as I go.

This is quite the opposite to others with a more linear and logical left-brain style. Instead, my natural intuition, imagination and creative flair give me an edge that is, in the main, deeply appreciated.

Finding each other through truth and kindness connects the individual journey with that of the group and community. When we open our hearts to another, we open a new level of transformation.

In the workplace, there is huge adversity and difficulty, and this is rarely discussed or shared. We push on and get on as the stress and pressure increases.

There are two ongoing choices for dealing with adversity: we may unconsciously re-enact our pain, therefore reinforcing it, or we can work through it consciously, unravelling the pain and breaking apart our patterns—returning to a fresh perspective.

- Our behaviour is not who we are but just an expression of how we are feeling.

The Power of Acknowledgment and Validation

My strength comes from this intuition plus my passion and courage to jump into the mess. In complex organisations, most people prefer to stand on the edge. In times of patient trouble on the acute psychiatric unit in New Zealand, the big burley nurses in charge would push me forward saying, "They won't hit Jenny!" However, I was cross with myself for being too brave when I stepped in too far and didn't dodge a large tray that came my way, creating a lump on my head as large as an egg!

My work is varied and always changing. There's no real magic to what I do. In essence, it is about providing a space in which people can talk, listen, be seen and understood. Processing problems and stepping out of the mess and into a better place requires acknowledgment, encouragement and validation. As human beings, we all need this to be at our best and understand who we are.

Being human is messy, but I don't mind that. From the life experience and training that I've received, there's not much pain, trouble and shame I can't handle. People come to me as they are, and I allow them to process their emotions and experiences and find answers within themselves.

- We all need a place to go to where we can ask questions. It's just easier to do it with a

sympathetic voice and with someone who
genuinely cares.

So, what are the practical methods that I use in my work as
a leadership coach?

1. A Space to Share What's Real
with no Blame or Shame

The Leadership Space is the official name I give to the place
where my clients solve problems, co-create and ultimately
achieve their goals. I combine a range of structural and
phenomenological approaches (phenomenology is the
philosophical study of the structures of experience and
consciousness). This might be one-to-one executive coaching,
group work or consultancy in wider organisational systems.

I work with people individually and in groups, but the
work and the space carry the same principles and structure.
The Team Leadership Space is designed for a group of any
size, generally 10 to 14, to come together for monthly sessions
over 6 to 12 months. We sit in a circle, which removes all
distractions and barriers as we are just left with ourselves.

- In this space, everyone has an equal place; there
  is no hierarchy. People sit where they like in the
  circle. Everyone is welcome to come as they are.

Because I deal with sensitive and serious issues, my work
needs protection and special attention. In all the work that
I do, I am meticulous about the space that people come

to, ensuring that they feel safe and at ease there. I call this the Leadership Space but it could equally be called the Human Space. Quite simply, my coaching interventions and unorthodox approach offer a respectfully held space for leaders and others to enter and share what's troubling them and what's causing their greatest problems so they can execute their intentions and deliver at their best. It's a place where people can bring themselves and their vulnerability.

- It is only when we feel safe and at ease that we relax and show our true selves.

When I sit with people, they are welcomed without judgement or shame. There are no expectations or hidden agendas, and all left-brain tasks are kept off the table. This basic principle of acceptance without expectation is often all we need to solve a problem. Within our jam-packed days and typical working patterns, it's hardly surprising when we don't come up with ideas and the innovations we need.

The point of entering a 'human space' with others is to share the experience of honesty and integrity and a true understanding of our deepest issues. With this comes compassion, connection and strength. When we get to the complexity of what keeps us awake at night, I see the most incredible things happen and, with these breakthroughs, comes change.

- Vulnerability = intimacy, the golden thread of connection.

In the past, I've been described as a workaholic (a bit harsh) and an achievement addict (almost as harsh). And, like many driven leaders, my quality of life has suffered. So, when I work with leaders and their teams who are under great pressure and stress, I can honestly say that I know what it's like. We all have troubles, unresolved issues and unanswered questions. But when we come together and share, we know we are all in the same boat. We not only heal together but also achieve together on a spectacular level.

As a coach, much of my work is quite simple: I listen, I see, I acknowledge and I validate people's existence. Regardless of colour, creed or status, I hear the same problems and issues. None of us is immune to workplace or life problems, and behind all the bravado and unpleasant behaviour lies a person experiencing hurt and unpleasant feelings which are preventing them from getting on with their dreams.

– When people realise that they are not alone
  in this, they relax about losing confidence
  and accept that they don't need to be
  superhuman and that it's okay not to be
  a perfectly formed machine.

2. The Leadership Looking Glass —Perspective is Everything

In my work I like to look at leadership issues through a series of lenses which give a deeper perspective, providing insight and increasing awareness, therefore getting to the root of problems and seeing how the different elements relate.

First there is the *Self-Leadership Lens*. Seeing ourselves as we truly are increases awareness and builds a deeper understanding of why we do the things we do. Knowing yourself is fundamental to developing as a leader and a human being and is a never-ending process. This lens eradicates blind spots and removes blocks, shows things differently and shines the light on limiting beliefs that are holding you back.

Second is the *Relational Lens*, the one that enables us to connect with others. We see how we work in our relationships, how we perceive others, interact with others, our biases and how we create shared possibilities and change. This lens examines dynamics, power games and how we can break the cycle of disempowerment, and it awakens the possibility of equality and shared growth.

Third we have the *Systemic Leadership Lens*. It's through this lens that we develop our systemic awareness and understanding at a higher level. This is essential for organisational shifts, market breakthroughs and staying ahead of the game. By seeing the parts of the system, known and unknown, from a hidden and higher perspective, we gain insight, and answers almost fall out of the sky. Much of my work is in this area as it is this more complex viewing of the system that holds the key to the most troubling issues that have worn us out for years.

For all these ways of looking, I have different methodologies, psychometrics and models. I will touch on a few within this chapter, but regardless of the method, it is only with perspective, context and awareness that we can move past denial, disbelief and defence and decide how we will deliver at our best.

– Once we see it, we can change.

3. Check in: Building Psychological Safety and Trust

Building a safe place for people to come to, and feel safe to express themselves freely in, is one of the most important elements of my work. Without safety and trust, there is no foundation to work from.

In the leadership space I hold, the leader is part of the team and can relax while I facilitate. The leader needs to come as they are with no expectation other than being part of the team. To build connections, safety and trust, we always start with a check-in, which enables people to feel welcome and at ease.

In the check-in we sit in a circle. There are no interruptions and people can take as long as they like to express themselves. This is a simple process, yet carefully managed so that people can voice what they like. Talking about feelings, thoughts and experiences without expectation quickly builds psychological safety and trust. It is this simplicity, structure and equality that allows people to open up.

As time goes on, and with experiences shared, people feel able to express their true selves. For this approach to be successful, the leader has to believe in the power of authenticity and collective voice and thought and, at the same time, be comfortable to be vulnerable and honest.

- The check-in is an essential platform for human connection and respect for all.

On many occasions this is so effective at generating freedom of speech and resolution to conflict that we never move past the first stage. I've worked with many teams that never had to go beyond this point as they've gained so much value and solved so many misunderstandings. What comes next depends on the group's intentions. I use a range of methods to gain answers to questions posed.

For any organisation taking leadership development seriously, I recommend that all members of the team have an individual coach and embark on a journey of personal growth. One-to-one coaching is extremely powerful for individual and leadership transformation.

Embarking on a journey of inner growth is not for the faint-hearted but worth every minute in my book. When you sit in a group, it's easier to dodge the bullets, paying lip service to the process.

When you are on 'the journey', you awaken yourself.

4. Dealing with Tough and Complex Issues —the Systemic Lens

Many of the people I work with are having to deal with tough and complex organisational and leadership issues. Alongside mainstream methods, I also use a relatively new approach: Business and Organisational Constellations (BOC). Both the mainstream methods I use and Business and Organisational Constellations are powerful ways to analyse complex problems and find innovative yet sustainable solutions.

BOC, in particular, is an excellent methodology through which to adopt a personal, relational and systemic lens and, in my experience, has the power to break through the most stubborn and unseen issues, often lifelong problems.

Business and Organisational Constellations is a form of Family Constellations, a therapeutic approach used to address personal issues and create balance in personal relationships devised by Bert Hellinger, a German psychotherapist. In the workplace, these methods are used to diagnose the root of complex and repetitive problems and help release any blocks—so opening the way for leaders to make intelligent and bold moves.

- It's like using a looking glass which sees the component parts that you couldn't spot with a human eye.

The process is simple, yet you need to be hugely skilled to facilitate this method, with a lot of practice and insight at a much higher level than with any traditional approach. A lot of senior leaders like this method because they haven't got much time and quite frankly don't care how they get to the answer they need. I have found that this method can be used in a number of ways: to gain insight into hidden issues, uncover historical and puzzling blocks, bring resolution and make management decisions about transformations such as mergers, reorganisations and strategy development.

- This methodology enables sense to be made from the most confusing matters which even the smartest leaders can't work out. The approach is quick and simple with great insight gained.

I work with leaders, teams and groups of people all over the world using this methodology, and it has helped many of my clients with system change at a significant level. I also use it to solve my own leadership and personal problems.

5. The Courage to See Our Wisdom

I have been blessed with the best teachers, coaches, mentors and friends to help me with my journey. I can honestly say, though, that self-reflection and my own intuition (and pain) is the greatest leadership teacher.

It's the mistakes I've made, learning the hard way, that have given me the knowledge to lead as I want to and be who I really am.

Most people I work with are super smart and have well-developed brains. Even the cleverest, however, benefit from sharpening their wisdom. Our intuition is the most powerful tool we have and, by making the implicit explicit, we can face what is true and real.

- By daring to look, we uncover blind spots and see the elephant in the room.

In a nutshell, my work is all about using what skill and knowledge I have with kindness, shining the light on blindness and gently uncovering the truth. Seeing what is real and digging through the dirt means looking in places we would rather not. Moving out of denial and into our innate wisdom requires courage and a lot of hard work on the part of everyone involved.

Intuition cannot exist alone, though. From the relationships we have with others comes the power of shared wisdom. We cannot live in isolation, and connection and companionship bring deep healing, innovation and fundamental change.

- Leadership can feel like a lonely path, but it cannot be conquered alone.

In my final chapter, I share my most recent leadership realisation and a solution to one of our biggest problems—feeling trapped, wanting to escape something (even from our own thoughts) and realising that the cage is actually open. It's just up to us to decide when to fly.

Lessons
1. Leadership is lonely. Human connection is a good antidote.
2. The truth is not fixed and being human is messy. Remain open to possibility and perspective.
3. Have the courage to use your intuition to aid problem solving and decision making.

CHAPTER 10

THE ROAD TO FREEDOM

Shake off the Shackles of the Past and Embrace the Future

Any last chapter marks the beginning of a new one. So, I will close this book with how I have embarked on my road to fun and freedom and a completely new life.

Anyone reading this must have, at some point, fancied a walk on the wild side. This is my favourite side and part of my DNA. My life has never been boring. It's been one full of adventure, including occasionally some morally questionable behaviour! (Back in the day, of course.) Through these pages, I hope that I've given a taste of what it takes to be onboard an occasionally slightly out-of-control bus.

In taking the road to freedom, you must be wild. But, with wildness, you must also be respectful and well-trained, and this journey is not for the faint-hearted. You have to be a brave and graceful warrior, have your wits about you and know when to fight, when to retreat and even when to hide. There are villains, robbers and even a few cowboys along the way. The name of the game is to keep your eye on the prize—your journey to the promised land of freedom.

All that Glitters
is not Gold

In my life, I've lost count of the times that I've been talked into a job, a relationship or buying that new shiny thing (that I didn't need). I was once described, unkindly, as a magpie (jumping on the next brand-new burnished bus), as well as being called fanatical and even mad as a hatter! I am certainly one for something lustrous, and I love a sparkly dream.

Pursuing the truth—whether gleaming or gloomy—has not caused me too many problems though. My passion is a strength. Even so, I've sometimes needed to rein in my naivety, which can get me into scrapes. But we must learn such lessons along the road to freedom. It is your path and does not belong to anyone else.

Write Your Own Story

Writing this book has provided its own freedom, and reflecting on my life has given me the opportunity to express myself with truth and respect. It could have been written from a different perspective, but it's been my freedom to choose. I choose to talk from a positive place because that is who I am. In compiling your story, it's your voice that matters, and if anyone wants to read it, that's entirely up to them.

After writing this book, I find I am now free of the need to please people or care what they might say. I've spent most of my life people-pleasing and compensating for the faults of others. My over-giving ways are no more. I am well on the road to being free of the relentless need to be accepted, loved, and being told I can belong only if I play by someone else's rules.

Escaping the Ghost Kingdom

"It is the Land of What Might Have Been.
It is the Land of the As if Dead..."
Betty Jean Lifton

Looking back on my life, and putting things mentally in their place, has helped me to find myself. In the lives of adoptees, it often takes them until they reach their forties or fifties to piece their lives together, to get a sense of who they are and to be satisfied with what they find. But with historical understanding plus emotional release comes freedom and peace of mind.

In the mind of an adopted child is the 'Ghost Kingdom'. This term was introduced in Betty Jean Lifton's book, *Journey of the Adopted Self* (Basic Books, 1994), as a place where the adopted child keeps the lost birth mother and birth father, and where his original self (the eternal ghost baby) is not able to grow up. The Ghost Kingdom is an alternative place, a portable home which adoptees carry inside them.

Many adopted children feel invisible or voiceless because they are forced to repress their need to know about their origins. They experience shame and a split loyalty after being taken into a new, loving family. They feel that an essential part of them is unacknowledged by their adoptive family and society as a whole because it is hidden, and no-one really wants to talk about it.

Every adopted child has experienced the trauma of being separated from his or her blood kin. It comes via a legal arrangement. Social workers feel it is politically correct to say that the birth mother has made an 'adoption plan'. Birth mothers, though, call it 'surrendering' the child. Nancy Verrier, an adoptive mother, calls it the 'primal wound' (also the title of her book, Gateway Press, 1993). Whatever language they use, adoptees feel the mother's disappearance as an abandonment.

The cumulative adoption trauma and the need to dissociate from feelings of loss, grief, and anger is something that all adoptees face.

Secretly grieving and squashing feelings, I didn't even think I deserved to have them. I didn't realise until recently, in my fifties, that my sense of self was incomplete. I couldn't quite place an entire part of me lost to this unacknowledged grief. This sense of incompleteness explains why many adoptees search for their birth mothers. It is a way of forming a coherent sense of self.

By integrating my past and present, I am now able to move on to the future and free myself from my ghosts. Seeing what is real and breaking the cycle of hoping for what does not exist is the biggest realisation and the one which has finally given me my freedom. You don't have to uphold someone else's delusion to survive, or fill in the gaps of one-sided relationships with you doing all the work.

From patterns of imagining and cycles of disappointment, I believed that my sense of self was tied up in someone else's approval. However, my road to freedom doesn't involve a begging bowl, or accepting crumbs from the table. Rather it means believing in myself.

Daring to be Free

A caged bird may choose to stay inside and never fly again, even when the door is opened. Many of us are like this: we don't like our cage but we don't want to fly, however bad things get. Often, we are more afraid of the unknown than a very uncomfortable current situation. In craving certainty, many of us don't take the leap and jump. True freedom can come at great cost.

Freedom comes in different forms to us all: what might be freedom to one would be a prison for another. When I spent over three months wandering around Southeast Asia doing what I liked, although this was a great adventure and I learnt some of my greatest lessons, oddly I didn't feel that free. I missed my friends and the routine and structure of normal life. There's sometimes freedom in familiarity.

Human beings are prediction machines. Our brains love nothing more than to follow patterns and habits. My mum, at 93, keeps going and stays happy because she knows what she's doing most of the day. Her brain can relax knowing that it's a cup of tea at 4pm and bed no later than 10. She doesn't like anything that disturbs this balance, and when we're all in chaos, she's sitting happily, wondering what all the fuss is about.

If I look at my own current freedoms, I seem to have quite a lot. But we all need to be sure that we haven't been conditioned like the caged bird and mistake the cage for comfort.

Despite the loss and pain brought by any great change, the upside is often our freedom. It might be a relationship, it might be a job or even a breakthrough moment which turns your life on a sixpence. For all the misery, there is nothing better than your own personal freedom, and it is always much closer than you realise. We are all so used to being trapped and afraid of escape that we kid ourselves that this is normal. Deep down, we know the world is out there. We might dream it, we might even plan for it, but the real freedom is taking the first step, or the big leap off the cliff.

What does it take to be free? Free from our past, free from our work or free from the demons inside us? Freedom from the negative thoughts and relationships that no longer serve us? Letting go of what is not working for us any more and replacing it with something new or nothing at all is one of the hardest things we can do—and that's exactly why most of us never do it.

Imagine that a job you've been doing for years is wearing you down and, in some cases, almost destroying your spirit. So, why don't you leave? What stops us making the decision to do something new? Imagine, too, a relationship that you enjoyed so much, in which you laughed, had fun and loved each other through and through. But the relationship is no longer serving you—with its constant arguments and you having to dodge more than a few nasty comments.

Waves and Wake-up Moments

You need to be ready to face the truth, but only when you feel safe to do so. Don't rush, be gentle and trust your heart to hold you. Admitting the pain and shame is hard and can repeat the original trauma. Hiding from it is smart and strategic safety behaviour. These are the instincts that keep us alive. Anyone who has experienced any trauma knows about survival behaviour and becomes a master at it. Pleasing people and having few, if any, demands, keeps us in the background and safe from any rejection or harm. So, when you think of facing the truth, make sure you surround yourself with people who see you and validate your experience.

Before writing this last chapter, I was confronted by the truth of a deeply hurtful period of rejection. But I was ready, and so the truth came. Trust your instincts and know that when your heart is strong, the road to freedom will open up right in front of you.

Freedom comes in waves, in wake-up moments and sometimes in little drips along the way. It comes from seeing the truth, processing pain and being alive to the possibility that it doesn't always have to be this way. As you grow and become more whole, you realise that you don't need what you needed before and are free to be as you please.

Walk Away from Threats
to Your Peace of Mind

This is a personal journey and your road only. People might join you and then leave you, but the person that always stays there is you. Don't expect to get well in the environment that made you ill, and know when to escape. Do something completely different. Break the pattern. You can't keep doing the same thing and expect to get a different result. Simple things like changing your hair colour or buying new shoes might even be a start.

Stop listening to what others think of you. That is their business not yours. Listen largely to what you think of yourself, and only seek validation from people that get you and have been down the road that you've travelled, or at least know what it's like.

Letting go of responsibility means divorcing yourself from having to fix everything and overly trying to please. Why do we hang on to the stuff that's bad for us? Even if we do let go of it, who are we? What are we without the ego? Our fear, our anger, our pain, our thoughts, our patterns, our habits. We must face the question: what are we when we are free of responsibility?

Maturity is having responsibility for yourself and walking away from the over-responsibility of others. Getting ready to fly is part of the road to freedom, and there are no shortcuts. Focus on your process and be honest about it. For example, cutting someone completely from your life is sometimes necessary for your health and peace of mind. But cutting the cord isn't always easy. We are all connected, after all.

Freedom From the Grip

If a situation comes along, let it. If it goes, let it. Don't make it a problem. You either accept a situation or deal with it. We often hang on to everything as if we own the answer and it is our problem alone to solve. This grip and inability to let go has been one of my problems and the challenge of many. It might be the grip of perfectionism, having to be right, proving a point or just not wanting to take part in something.

The grip of anything that gets you is the grip that you need to release. This could be fear, terror or your ruminating thoughts—the ones that won't leave you and keep knocking at the door; the unhealthy obsessions that keep telling you that you have no control; another person's power over you; a job that you've done for years but you know is no longer good for you.

My quest for belonging and love included positive illusion and self-deception—I convinced myself that things were better than they were, and that meant that I didn't let go of things early enough and got hurt. But the paradox of the Pollyanna principle is that when you let go of attachments and fixed beliefs, you live in more love and peace.

It's been a long road for me, but I now walk away from anything that is not good for me. I no longer put up with things, pick up other people's dirty litter, feel others' pain, take too much on or carry someone else's burden. But, most of all, I no longer live in a world of self-deception.

I let go, let be and let in what is good for me. I've let go of my need to be heard, right or just to have the final say.

I no longer waste my energy convincing people who were never interested anyway. Why waste your time persuading others that you are good, smart or brave? Be free from the need to justify yourself in places where you will never be understood or believed. It is a false hope and a total illusion to try continually to convince people of your opinions because you think that might give you some release. Talk to those you want to and share with the people you trust and in the relationships that matter to you.

Don't Rely on Others
for Your Happiness

Real freedom comes when fear, pain and rejection are replaced by true love. For all of us who have been rejected and told to go away, you're only being told that you're not needed in that person's life at that moment.

And here we have the biggest release of all: the freedom from the ridiculous thought that we need anyone. Having needs isolates you and takes away your power—whether it's the need to be married, have a guru, a religion or a teacher, or a fancy badge to prove something. You might quite like these things, but do you really need them? When we get too reliant on others, objects or ideas, they become addictions—and addictions weaken us.

All these things that you think you need are mainly distractions from the real truth: that you can only rely on yourself.

Believing that others need us just perpetuates the inflated opinion that you really matter that much. As parents, we think we have a right to tell our children what to do, even as they grow up. But this is ignoring their right to have a life that they choose. The little caged birds need to fly away. We may miss them, their songs and their lovely feathers, but who's to say they won't cope—and thrive?

Changing Your Life Requires a Determined Mind

Nothing lasts forever, however painful or pleasurable. We all know that the primary cause of unhappiness is not the situation itself but our thoughts about it.

A wise man once said: "A disciplined mind leads to happiness, and an undisciplined mind leads to suffering." So let's be disciplined and secure freedom from the bad stuff and become acquainted with the good.

A wise woman once said: "Have a determined mind and never give up on your dreams."

So let's be determined and go for the prize.

Final Thoughts

- Don't try to be someone you're not.
- Don't hurt anyone along the way, and certainly don't let anyone hurt you.
- Lead your life and let others lead theirs.
- Keep reaching within and believing in yourself.
- It's never too late to change the road that you're on, no matter how far you've travelled

Lastly, a word to the teachers: thank you to all my teachers, the nice ones, the nasty ones, the ones that I'd rather not have had. We don't really get to choose our teachers. You don't know why they come and what form they will take. But they are all there for a reason, and it is up to us to learn the lesson. And they will just keep coming until the lessons have been learnt.

Have I reached the end of the road? Not at all. Am I on the right bus, in the right lane and on the road to freedom? Yes, I certainly am. Regardless of the bus you're on, make sure you enjoy the ride because you never know if it's the last one or if there's another one just behind.

POSTSCRIPT

The Freedom Bus Awaits

When David and I were sitting eating our dinner last night, we looked at each other and agreed that we were both completely different from the people we were when we met.

The years can change you. They age you physically, undoubtedly, but we feel younger and happier than ever.

Together we have made it through some of the best and most difficult years of our lives.

With all the love and romance, we also have had to find our way and carve our path, and this has not been without argument and reluctantly backing down (well, David has at least!).

What with my impulsive nature and David's overly critical nature, we are really doing quite well.

So now for my next adventure. My Freedom Bus awaits. What will the next chapter be? I really don't have a clue.

Three Final Lessons
1. Make peace with your past.
2. Make sense of your present.
3. Make a dream for your future.

And if you don't do any of these, at least make yourself happy by being your true self.

140

ABOUT THE AUTHOR

Jenny Rossiter is one of the UK's leading executive coaches, supporting leaders and their teams. She has had over 27 years' experience in the pharmaceutical and biotech industry, and has worked with numerous leaders in this field.

Jenny's mission is to bring humanity into business, and this enables her to get to the heart of the matter quickly and solve complex problems with compassion and understanding.

She believes that raising the bar of leadership, through building gold-standard behaviour, creates an environment in which organisations can achieve and everyone is proud of who they are.

Jenny has a passion for weaving together real human experience with practical, science-based techniques. Her deep understanding of human behaviour draws parallels between issues raised on the psychiatric wards and in the corporate battleground.

She combines her expertise in neuroleadership, dispute resolution and emotional intelligence to help leaders and their teams tackle some of the biggest business taboos. With a new focus on neurodiversity in the workplace, Jenny aims for *difference* to be accepted and embraced—and even respected as the new *superpower.*